THE M & E HANDBOOK SERIES

Public Administration

Michael P. Barber
LLB (LOND), DPA (LOND)
Senior Lecturer at the Brighton Polytechnic

SECOND EDITION

MACDONALD AND EVANS

Macdonald and Evans Ltd.
Estover, Plymouth PL6 7PZ

First published 1972
Reprinted 1974
Reprinted 1975
Second edition 1978

© Macdonald and Evans Ltd. 1978

7121 1685 0

Phototypeset in V.I.P. Times by
Western Printing Services Ltd, Bristol
Printed in Great Britain by
Hazell Watson & Viney
Aylesbury, Bucks

M & E HANDBOOKS

M & E Handbooks are recommended reading for examination syllabuses all over the world. Because each Handbook covers its subject clearly and concisely books in the series form a vital part of many college, university, school and home study courses.

Handbooks contain detailed information stripped of unnecessary padding, making each title a comprehensive self-tuition course. They are amplified with numerous self-testing questions in the form of Progress Tests at the end of each chapter, each text-referenced for easy checking. Every Handbook closes with an appendix which advises on examination technique. For all these reasons, Handbooks are ideal for pre-examination revision.

The handy pocket-book size and competitive price make Handbooks the perfect choice for anyone who wants to grasp the essentials of a subject quickly and easily.

Preface

The object of this HANDBOOK is to provide a guide to the study of British public administration which will not only explain the theoretical and structural aspects of the system, but will also attempt to show the problems facing contemporary public administration. The HANDBOOK attempts to deal with both the theory and practice of public administration, and places emphasis on the current "management" approach to the subject.

The HANDBOOK is intended principally for students studying for the examinations of the Local Government Examinations Board, for the Diploma in Public Administration of the University of London, for the National Certificate examinations in Public Administration and for the BEC higher level courses. This book is not intended completely to replace textbooks on the subject, but attempts to provide in one work a range of topics which a student would normally only study by having recourse to a wide range of publications. It does not claim, however, to be exhaustive, and it is doubted whether any single book could fill the needs of a student in this vast and constantly changing subject. It is thus confidently expected that students will supplement their studies by experience gained in their employment, especially as regards the day-to-day working of the system, and by reading widely. In particular, useful articles appear regularly in the *Political Quarterly*, *Public Administration* and *Public Law*. This book deals mainly with central administration, and students are therefore strongly recommended to supplement their study by reference to the HANDBOOK on *Local Government*.

September 1978

M.P.B.

Contents

CHAPTER I

The Nature of Public Administration

1. What is public administration? Public administration has been defined as "... decision-making, planning the work to be done, formulating objectives and goals ... establishing and reviewing organisations, directing and supervising employees ... exercising controls and other functions performed by government executives and supervisors. It is the action part of government; the means by which the purposes and goals of government are realised". (Corson and Harris, *Public Administration in Modern Society*, McGraw-Hill, 1969.)

Public administration thus is basically the administrative side of government as opposed to the legislative and judicial sides. This view, however, must be examined in the light of the impossibility of distinguishing conceptually between these functions of government in any conclusive manner, and, as will be seen, the administration effectively exercises what can properly be classified as legislative functions (*see* V).

2. Framework of study. This HANDBOOK attempts a *critical approach* to the wide subject of public administration. In doing so it runs the risk of understating many virtues of British government in its attempt to isolate the effective issues of efficiency from those of tradition, etc. In an age of reform in all spheres, however, such an approach is justified in order to avoid falling into the approach epitomised by Swift, who commented, "I would hide the frailties and deformities of my political mother, and place her virtues and beauties in the most advantageous light".

The approach to public administration thus involves a study of the principal problem areas in the subject and also illustrates the scope of public administration. This includes the following topics.

(*a*) The political and constitutional environment of public administration (*see* II).

(*b*) Organisational theory and government organisation (*see* III).

(*c*) Administrative processes such as planning, decision-making, co-ordination, etc. (*see* IV, V and X).

(*d*) Public service—characteristics, personnel, problems, etc. (*see* VI).

(*e*) Central and local financial administration (*see* VIII–IX).

(*f*) Control of administration (*see* II, XIV and XV).

(*g*) The relation of non-central government bodies, e.g. local authorities and public corporations (*see* XII and XIII).

3. Problems in the study of public administration. Problems associated with the study of public administration may be classified as those of principle, those associated with the overall governmental context, and those of a more particularly administrative nature.

4. Problems of principle. The following points should be noted.

(*a*) *Efficiency.* "In the science of administration, whether public or private, the basic 'good' is efficiency. The fundamental objective of the science of administration is least expenditure of manpower and materials. Efficiency is thus axiom number one in the value scale of administration" (Luther Gulick, *Papers on the Science of Administration*, Inst. of Public Administration, New York, 1937).

However, in interpreting efficiency in public administration, cost yardsticks are not always available, nor are they always appropriate. Thus against the pure dictates of efficiency must be set the often competing factors of "public service", accountability, social responsibility, etc. Thus a new definition of efficiency is required for public administration.

(*b*) *Public context.* Decision-making in public administration is not an autonomous isolated function which can be imposed on "consumers", but is acted upon by forces transcending the individual context of the decision, and arises out of the interaction of social forces. As such, public administration decision-making is the product of non-commercial factors, and is constantly exposed to public criticism and review.

(*c*) *Political context.* Public administration operates in an essentially political environment. Not only is it subject (at least in theory) to political control, but decision by non-political administrators themselves involve both human judgment and a "political" element, although this political element does not take the form of "partisanship". It arises in that the final sanction of the decision lies in accountability and responsibility to the elected political representatives, and thus the nature of a decision must reflect this responsibility.

(d) *Governmental powers*. These are absolute powers; the powers of taxation, coercion, etc., are matters of politics rather than economic and administrative convenience.

NOTE: Thus the principles present problems basic to public administration in relation to the meaning of administrative efficiency, the nature of administrative decisions and the nature of the environment within which the administration operates.

5. Problems in the overall government context. The role and functioning of public administration must be set in the context of the problems confronting government, which are as follows:

(a) The reconciliation of liberty with the duty to govern. The government must be strong enough to command obedience and to administer effectively, whilst at the same time being controlled in order to establish responsibility to certain standards, i.e. the conflict between sovereignty and responsibility.

(b) The need to balance achievement of the common good with the demands of vested interests.

(c) The balance of present necessities with future desirabilities.

(d) The need to balance traditional attitudes with scientific curiosity.

6. Administrative problems. On the practical administrative plane particular problems of public administration arise. These were classified by Finer as:

(a) the machinery for co-ordination;
(b) the principles of departmentalisation;
(c) the accountability of the executive to the courts and parliament;
(d) the provision of expert knowledge;
(e) the recruitment and maintenance of qualified personnel in the public services.

Although these are major areas of study they tend to obscure problems revealed by the modern science of administration. In consequence, it is necessary to add such areas as organisational theory, organisational behaviour, decision-making, planning, etc.

7. Changes in governmental functions. The role of the state has developed from that of a mere "nightwatchman", exercising relatively minor regulatory functions (i.e. a negative approach) to that of a positive interventionist and active planning role. This change has manifested itself from a public administration stand-point in the growth of a centralist, hierarchical and professionalised administrative machine.

8. Causes of the change. Underlying factors which have led to this change in the role of the state include the following.

(*a*) The rise of organised labour, particularly since the end of the First World War, with its attendant demands for security and the establishment and preservation of national minimum standards. This manifests itself politically through increased demands for state intervention.

(*b*) The concentration of capital and the consequent demands of industry for intervention from a promotional aspect.

NOTE: Thus forces of protection and promotion have interacted effectively to end economic liberalism.

(*c*) The greater division of labour and the consequent realisation that various units in the economy are in fact interdependent. Thus state intervention is needed to protect and advance the weaker elements, e.g. through regional economic planning (*see* X).

(*d*) Improved communications which have increased the scope of the state's role and consequently reduced the need for local units of administration.

(*e*) The demand for efficiency in government, which has required, in practice, more specific and positive government.

(*f*) Technological developments, which in themselves have led to the need for increased government involvement and regulation, e.g. increased car ownership has produced attendant traffic and environmental problems.

(*g*) The concept of environmental protection which may well operate as a contemporary influence on government intervention in order to prevent private exploitation and damage in this field.

9. Some effects of administrative growth. The growth in size and functions of the government and administrative machine has had certain side results apart from problems directly associated with the growth, e.g. organisational and co-ordination problems. These problems are threefold:

(a) the alienation of the individual from the decision-making process (see XV);

(b) difficulties existing in establishing the "public will";

(c) problems of general direction or overall nature of the role of the state are accentuated, e.g. between an interventionist or *laissez-faire* approach.

10. Factors affecting the direction of government. Before any specific matters of party political controversy arise there are certain factors in existence which affect the general direction of a government.

(a) Cultural attitudes both affect the direction of government in a positive sense, and also operate negatively to limit the activities of government. In the former case, for example, it will manifest itself in community attitudes towards the provision of basic services and, in the latter case, values and beliefs held by the community will operate to define boundaries between that which is considered to be in the political sphere and that which is an inappropriate area for anything other than peripheral government involvement.

NOTE: Although cultural attitudes have effects these are naturally general and such matters as the precise limits of government involvement will be a political matter.

(b) The general British belief in gradual evolution of government and society as opposed to alterations based solely on pragmatic reasoning, whilst retarding the speed of change, operates to reduce resistance to change when it does take place.

(c) The "cultural mix" in British society prevents deep social and class distinctions and produces a general consensus approach to many functions of government.

11. Public administration and private business. In III we deal with the difficulties of applying theories of management organisation to public administration where such theories are founded on research in the private sector. However, the following distinguishing factors between public administration and private business must be borne in mind from the outset.

(*a*) *Political environment*. Public administration operates within the environment of a political system in which governments are, in principle, required to operate as impartial arbiters between competing interests in society. In consequence:

(*i*) the government creates individual rights and imposes constraints on individual and group behaviour;

(*ii*) the administrator is in frequent contact with his clients and his major concern is with equity and impartiality;

(*iii*) administrative procedures are built around strict compliance with the law.

On the other hand private industry is essentially guided by the principle of maximisation of profits and does not act as an arbiter between conflicting social interests.

(*b*) *Social costs*. Public administration decision-making varies from that of private business in that where private business is concerned primarily with questions of financial cost and benefit, public administration is intimately concerned with concepts of social costs and benefits in addition to those of a mere financial nature.

(*c*) *Public interest*. Public administration is often evaluated by its ability to operate in a manner so as to maximise and integrate the public interest, whereas private business is evaluated on the basis of profit maximisation. In practice this makes it much more difficult to quantify in financial terms the substantial investment of resources undertaken by the public sector.

(*d*) *Instability*. As a result of operating in a political environment public administrators are faced with a much greater turnover of political leadership and consequent changes in policy than is encountered in private business.

(*e*) *Allocation of responsibilities*. The method of allocation of functions in the public sector is often based more on political considerations than on pure tests of efficiency.

(*f*) *Planning*. Owing to the pressures of political scrutiny public administrators spend a greater proportion of their time on short-term measures than does the equivalent management level in private industry.

(*g*) *Functions*. Public administration is faced with a much wider variety of functions than those operating in private business, and also deals with matters which are the exclusive province of central administration, e.g. defence, and law and order.

12. Politics and administration. "In the sense that politics has to do with making government generally acceptable through the interplay of multiple interests, ideas and ideals in relation to government courses of action, even very lowly employees of government have at least an indirect part in it. . . . The higher one goes in government, the greater the involvement in politics because of involvement in greater public concerns" (Paul H. Appleby, *Public Administration for a Welfare State*).

However, this involvement of administrators in politics is not to be construed as involvement in party politics and certain important differences exist between politicians and administrators, namely:

(*a*) politicians are tied to political parties;
(*b*) a difference is also found at the level of responsibility, i.e. between the intra-organisational responsibility of the administrator and the party and wider public responsibility of the politician.

Nevertheless it must be emphasised that civil servants wield considerable political power, in the sense that "political" is equated with the decision-making function as opposed to the notion of partisanship, and are a vital part of the political system of the country. Civil servants have technical and political roles, this point being developed in VI.

13. Policy and administration. A particular fallacy in public administration is that view which holds that policy-making and administration can be either conceptually or practically separated. This matter is dealt with in V, where it is shown that in fact administrators make policy within the very general framework of goals by political parties.

PROGRESS TEST 1

1. What special problems are involved in the study of public administration? (3–6)
2. Why, and how, has the role of the state changed in the twentieth century?   (7–10)
3. Distinguish between public and private administration. (11)
4. Distinguish between politics and administration. (12)

CHAPTER II

The Constitutional Framework of Public Administration

INTRODUCTION

The British governmental system differs markedly when in operation from the role laid down for it in constitutional theory. This affects both the operation of, and the attitudes towards, public administration. In particular the purist doctrine of demarcation between legislative and executive functions no longer obtains and the relative functions and powers of these organs of government must be examined in the light of the increasing domination of the executive branch. Further, the concept of the three traditional organs of government, namely, the legislature, the executive and the judiciary, may be extended to four by adding administration, in the form of a full-time professional civil service, wielding independent power and influence in the field of policy-making (*see* V).

1. Some characteristics of the British system. Some of the more important, as opposed to merely more traditional, characteristics of British government may be classified as follows.

(*a*) *Responsible government*. The British governmental system may be regarded as a system of responsible government to the extent that such responsibility is manifested through the doctrine of ministerial responsibility (*see* XV) and collective Cabinet responsibility (*see* 17). It is through the practical operation of these doctrines that responsibility to Parliament and through Parliament to the electorate is achieved in respect of the administration of government.

(*b*) *Cabinet government*. In so far as Parliament is effectively dominated by the Cabinet (*see* 5–7) the British system may be treated as having effectively moved from a system of parliamentary to Cabinet government.

"In the cabinet are found the modern embodiment of a fusion of governmental powers which, more than the eighteenth century separation, has generally characterised British government" (G.C. Moodie, *The Government of Great Britain*, 1967).

(*c*) *Two-party system*. Britain effectively operates under a two-party system of government. Both the main parties are relatively homogeneous in terms of policy. They effectively organise the House of Commons, provide and sustain governments, and serve as vital links between government and the electorate. They thus arose as organisers and informers after the extension of the franchise.

(*d*) *Conventions*. The absence of exhaustive constitutional law has resulted in a consequent reliance on unwritten conventions (*see* 11–15) and these conventions serve to regulate the exercise of power to a much greater extent than formal machinery.

2. The doctrine of separation of powers. The underlying premise adopted by advocates of constitutional government is the necessity of establishing a system which at the same time as recognising the role of government in society provides machinery whereby such government is brought under popular control, and limits are placed on the exercise of power. One of the concepts at the basis of this philosophy is the doctrine of the separation of powers which, though not largely accepted, provides a form of measurement against which systems of government can be measured. In practice the simple doctrine, which has of itself never provided an effective constitutional basis, has been combined with other doctrines, e.g. of mixed government, and of "checks and balances" (as in the U.S.A.). In particular the old approach to separation of powers is not appropriate to the twentieth century with its increasing emphasis on administrative power, and the narrowing of the old emphasis from that of legislature and government to that between the political branch of government and the bureaucratic part.

3. The doctrine in Great Britain and the U.S.A. As expounded by Montesquieu, one of its essentials for liberty was that each of the three branches of government should be confined to the exercise of its own allotted functions and not allowed to encroach upon the functions of the other branches. Additionally individuals should not be members of more than one branch. This, according to the theory, would prevent one branch gaining domination. This approach has never been achieved in Great Britain, though it has been more nearly approached in the U.S.A. with its separation of legislative and executive personnel and the mutual checks and balances operating between these. The doctrine in Great Britain is considerably diverged from in executive and legislative relations. (For the purpose of this chapter the independence of the judiciary can be accepted subject to the encroachment of administrative tribunals (*see* XIV).)

4. Legislature and executive relations. The doctrine of parliamentary sovereignty (i.e. that there are no legal constraints upon the will of Parliament), must be regarded as operating through, and to the benefit of, the domination by government of Parliament.

By convention, members of the government must be members of one or other House of Parliament and invariably, in practice, leading members are members of the House of Commons. Thus the majority party in Parliament not only provides the government but is also effectively required to support the government. Theoretically it may also dismiss a government, though the likelihood of this occurring in anything other than abnormal conditions, e.g. absence of majority governments or wartime conditions, are extremely remote. The government, particularly through the Cabinet which consists of the principal government office-holders and consequently the political leaders of the majority party, is in a position, through reliance on this support, to determine what legislation shall be presented to Parliament, and thus to reduce Parliament to the status of a purely critical body.

5. How is this domination achieved? The factors contributing to Cabinet domination of Parliament, and thus to the effective system of Cabinet rather than parliamentary government, are as follows.

(*a*) *Party discipline*. The punitive authority of party over individuals is manifested ultimately through "withdrawal of the party ticket" for failure to conform. This disciplinary element tends to be overrated in practice and allegiance may better be regarded from the conformatory aspect.

(*b*) *Party loyalty*. The adherence of party members to the broad principles and strategies of their party results in the likelihood of their conforming to government programmes even though they may be against certain aspects of these. This response can be illustrated by the fate of revolts against the party whip which reveals that these are generally stage-managed in order to register dissent without defeat, e.g. the Labour back-bench revolt over entry to the E.E.C.

(*c*) *Self-interest*. The fear of M.P.s that defeat and /or dissolution will endanger their personal constituency majorities and will involve them in unwanted electioneering is a powerful incentive to conform. In addition the increase in the number of government posts provides incentives to regular "party-liners".

6. Effect of domination. The major effects are as follows.

(*a*) The Cabinet has effective control of the parliamentary timetable and private members are in consequence subordinated to the pressures of business chosen by the government.

(*b*) The Cabinet determines the programme of policy to be presented to Parliament in the form of legislation.

(*c*) Parliament takes on a non-legislative role and emphasis thus must be placed upon, and any discussion of its effectiveness must centre on, its ability to exercise its critical function (*see* **21** below).

THE CABINET

7. The Cabinet in the British constitution. The report of the Committee on the Machinery of Government (the Haldane Committee), 1918, classified the function of the Cabinet as follows.

(*a*) The final determination of the policy to be submitted to Parliament.

NOTE: The interrelationship of the Cabinet and the bureaucracy in the exercise of this function is dealt with in V.

(*b*) The supreme control of the national executive in accordance with the policy prescribed by Parliament.

(*c*) The continuous co-ordination and delimitation of the authorities of the several departments of the state.

NOTE: This co-ordinative function and the machinery adopted for its exercise are dealt with in IV.

8. Problems of the Cabinet's legislative role. Three principal organisational problems have confronted the Cabinet in this sphere.

(*a*) Reconciliation of the political ambitions of its members.

(*b*) Organisation of work load and support services.

(*c*) Distillation of actual policy from individual views.

The second problem is facilitated by the development of Cabinet committees and the use of the Cabinet Secretariat, and by the further concentration of power in the hands of the Prime Minister (*see* **10**) and his inner Cabinet.

Cabinet committees (*see* IV) operate to discuss in advance matters destined for the full Cabinet, and give interested parties the opportunity to bargain and compromise.

The decisions of the Cabinet and sub-committees, the compilation of agenda, the circulation of memoranda, etc., are in the hands of the Cabinet Secretariat (*see* IV) which, though theoretically a recording agency, has vital co-ordinative functions.

9. Limitations upon the Cabinet. These are principally the following.

(*a*) The ability of the administrative machine effectively to execute Cabinet policy.

(*b*) The need to justify policies before Parliament, and the consequent need to make concessions.

10. Position of the Prime Minister. Any discussion of the significance of the Cabinet in public administration would be incomplete without an explanation of the role of the Prime Minister and in particular his movement from one of *primus inter pares* to one of effective authority. Commentators nowadays in fact tend to speak of a transition from Cabinet government to one of prime ministerial government. Ignoring personality factors, the reasons for the Prime Minister's domination may be classified as follows.

(*a*) The growth in the size of governments, giving the Prime Minister the power of patronage with obedience and acquiescence as the price of a job.

(*b*) Focus of the electoral system and its attendant publicity on the Prime Minister.

(*c*) The burden of departmental duties on other ministers, with the consequent tendency for policy-making responsibility to be concentrated in the hands of the Prime Minister.

(*d*) The prestige of the position.

(*e*) The power of dissolution and of choice, therefore, of election date.

CONVENTIONS

11. Nature of conventions. Conventions are at the centre of the adaptability and the representative and responsible character of British government. Their presence, however, is not limited to unwritten constitutions such as the British constitution, and they develop in any constitution in response to political needs, the inadequacy of formal rules, etc. Conventions have been formally defined as: "certain rules of constitutional behaviour which are considered to be binding by and upon those who operate the constitution, but which are not enforceable by law courts, nor by the presiding officers in the Houses of Parliament" (Marshall, G. and Moodie, G. C., *Some Problems of the Constitution*, Hutchinson, 1967).

12. Reasons for the existence of conventions. These are as follows.

(*a*) The inability of any rule of law to be self-applying, and the consequent need for informal rules to provide this element of adaptability.

(*b*) The difficulty in changing political and social circumstances, or eradicating doubts as to the interpretation of formal rules by adjudication or legislation.

(*c*) The need to legislate for certain aspects of political behaviour which are not formally legislatable.

13. Associated problems. In certain cases conventions may be readily definable, e.g. in the field of Commonwealth relations. In other cases, however, problems of establishing conventions may arise, namely:

(*a*) confusion between what is a prescriptive convention and what is merely a descriptive usage, e.g. the practice of consulting interested parties in the drafting of legislation;

(*b*) determination of the context of a particular convention and its applicability to particular circumstances;

(*c*) the lack of formal adjudicatory machinery for determining the existence of a convention: in particular, the essence of a convention, i.e. its acceptance as binding, may arise as the result of a misunderstanding in a particular case, or may not be regarded as binding by all parties concerned;

(*d*) the relation and necessity of precedents in the establishment of conventions.

14. Obedience to conventions. The absence of formal sanctions for breach of a rule tempts one to think that obedience to the rule is merely permissive. This view does not accord, however, with legal reality; laws are obeyed for reasons other than mere legal sanction, e.g. social pressures, moral attitudes, respect for law, etc. Why, then, are conventions obeyed? The following reasons may be suggested.

(*a*) Dicey's view that breach of a convention would lead to a breach of law is not all-embracing and only applies to certain conventions.

(*b*) Political difficulties might well be the result of a breach of a convention in that such a breach may destroy respect for constitutional practices or could lead to a change in the established balance of political powers.

(*c*) Respect for constitutional practices. A government is by convention required to resign if defeated on a major issue in the Commons. Its resignation may well then be a result of respect for the need to treat such a vote as a manifestation of the public will, as in practice there is no necessary reason to assume that it could not command support for the rest of its policies.

(*d*) Convenience and the desire to be accorded the same privileges, etc., oneself (when, for example, in opposition).

15. Examples of conventions. For detailed consideration of the principal examples, readers are advised to consult a work on constitutional law. Broadly and briefly, however, these may be stated as:

(*a*) the doctrines of ministerial and collective responsibility;

(*b*) conventions regarding the formation and resignation of governments;

(*c*) constitution of committees;

(*d*) accordance of rights to opposition parties, etc.

16. Ministerial responsibility. "Ministers are responsible *for* the general conduct of government, including the exercise of many powers legally vested in the monarch; and they are responsible *to* Parliament immediately and ultimately, through Parliament and parties, to the electorate" (G. Marshall and G. C. Moodie, *see* 11). In practice, ministerial responsibility is not clear-cut and presents problems both as to the definition of its substance and as regards the means by which Parliament is able to secure such responsibility. Responsibility means accountability, but in practice seems to have little punitive effect. In addition, it has certain undesirable side effects to the extent that it protects individual culpable civil servants.

17. Collective responsibility. This is an even looser concept and effectively means that a government must submit its policy as a whole to Parliament and must resign if unable to secure acceptance thereof. Looked at from another aspect it means that a minister who is individually unable to accept government policy must resign, e.g. as did Mr Frank Cousins in 1966 as a result of his disagreement with the government's Prices and Incomes Bill.

18. Safeguards of tradition. The theoretical interdependence of Parliament and the executive in practice gives way to executive primacy. As long as the executive can maintain majority support in Parliament it has the power to force any policy through Parliament. Before dealing with practical safeguards and controls of public administration, it is important to realise the underlying role of tradition in British governmental practice. A basic consensus of political beliefs exists in Britain which effectively prevents complete subjugation of Parliament by the executive. Some of these are the protection of minorities in debates by the Speaker, recognition and accordance of powers to the opposition, methods of constituting committees and activities and institutionalising of pressure groups (*see* XV).

These informal and intangible influences are at the basis of the constitution and their absence has proved disastrous in attempts to export the British constitution to states without these underlying factors, e.g. Nigeria.

NOTE: There is, however, a danger in over-reliance on these traditional safeguards and a tendency to use them to justify a lack of attention to formal machinery. As has been shown, the traditional consensus may break down, e.g. in the retrospective legislative overruling of the decision in *Burmah Oil Company* v. *Lord Advocate* (1964).

THE HOUSE OF COMMONS

19. Criticism. It has been commented that "there is much contemporary evidence to suggest that Britain so lacks effective scrutiny of the executive that a situation is created in which popular esteem for Parliament and government declines and its own effectiveness crumbles" (B. Crick, *The Reform of Parliament*. Weidenfeld Nicolson, 1972).

20. Basic factors in the relationship between Parliament and government. The major factors to be considered are as follows.

(*a*) Strong government and strong opposition are not incompatible. Executive domination of Parliament is probably necessary to facilitate the pushing through of legislative programmes. However, effective scrutiny and constructive criticism can improve policies and ensure that they represent public opinion.

(*b*) Parliament remains the most effective scrutinising body, and reliance on both the courts and the press as checks on the administration are inadequate.

(*c*) Checks and balances do not develop and modify in order to preserve the traditional relationship of interdependence.

(*d*) The two-party system does not result in inevitable alternations in governments and thus the sanction of quinquennial elections on its own is an inadequate check.

21. Parliament's role. The House of Commons has changed from a "legislative" body to a "legitimising" body, the old belief in the dichotomy between politics and administration having broken down. However, despite the decline into insignificance of the positive legislative role of the House, it still performs certain vital functions, especially concerning control of the executive, as follows.

(*a*) *Legitimising*. Parliament is not a mere rubber-stamp for government legislation. It involves publicity, debate, criticism, etc.

NOTE: This function may be curtailed by use of such machinery as the guillotine (as in the Industrial Relations Bill (1971) and the Wales Bill and Scotland Bill (1978)). However, the importance of such machinery can be overrated, as it is doubtful whether the true function of the House is discussion of detail (committee stage) anyway, as opposed to criticism of policy (at second reading stage).

(*b*) *Raising and discussing complaints and grievances*. This is nowadays the crucial traditional function of Parliament. It involves constant examination and criticism of governments. Although a government may confidently expect support from its parliamentary majority, the value of this critical function will be eroded if the government fails to make available sufficient information upon which criticism may be constructively based.

(c) *Control of the executive.* This is principally a matter of politics rather than of law. The ultimate deterrent of the vote is inadequate (*see* 6). However, governments may be induced to respond to parliamentary criticism where publicity is widely given to such criticisms or where morale of government supporters is undermined. Parliament can thus exercise control by making the government aware of the underlying drifts of public opinion.

NOTE: Control in practice does not mean coercive control but is more indicative of advice, scrutiny, publicity, etc. It is thus important in the control of the executive that Parliament develops machinery which is able to bring about informed criticism and consequent publicity, rather than machinery which will result in inherently weak and unstable government.

THE PARLIAMENTARY COMMITTEE SYSTEM

22. Introduction. It is through effective use of the committee system that parliamentary control of the executive is likely to be most effectively developed. In order to achieve effective control through committees it is desirable that the following conditions are satisfied.

(a) Committees should be as small as possible.

(b) There should be a precise definition of their functions and powers.

(c) Committees should be given as much time as possible.

(d) The committee should contain technical experts or should have ready access to them.

23. Evidence of Parliament group. The committee in its evidence to the Select Committee on Procedure considered that "the main weakness in Parliament's method of scrutinising administration, and indeed of debating policy matters, is the limited ability to obtain background facts and understanding essential for any detailed criticism of administration or any informed discussion of policy." It consequently recommended the following:

(*a*) that sub-committees of the Select Committee on Estimates should be organised along specialist lines (*see* VIII);

(*b*) that specialist committees were needed "to scrutinise the actions of government in their own fields and to collect, discuss, and report evidence relevant to proceedings in Parliament, whether legislative or other".

NOTE: The only specialised committee existing at the time was the Select Committee on Nationalised Industries.

24. Types of committee. The main types of committee are as follows.

(*a*) *Committees of the whole House.* These are not adequate forms for control of the executive but are of a more constitutional and representative character.

(*b*) *General standing committees.* These generally have no executive powers; they cannot summon persons, have no research staff and only "fortuitous" expertise, and cannot discuss matters outside the actual text of Bills presented to them. They thus perform only a limited control function.

(*c*) *Specialised standing committees.* These may be *ad hoc* or permanent. The more important of these are the Select Committee on Expenditure, the Public Accounts Committee (*see* X), the Select Committee on Nationalised Industries (*see* XV) and the Select Committee on Statutory Instruments.

25. Criticisms of the committee system. As instruments for controlling the executive the present committee system in general suffers from the following defects:

(*a*) failure to achieve adequate specialised enquiry into the activities of departments and various aspects of government policy;

(*b*) lack of specialised probing committees;

(*c*) the fact that standing committees as legislative entities do not represent a permanent specialised element in the committee system.

26. Arguments in favour of specialised committees. These are as follows:

(*a*) expert views can be developed through continuous service on one committee dealing with a single subject area;

(*b*) they develop the knowledge and critical powers of M.P.s;

(*c*) they provide a training function for potential ministers;

(*d*) the executive would benefit from criticism from more informed M.P.s;

(*e*) they represent the natural and logical extension of the need to delegate critical and investigatory powers;

(*f*) they could cut across party lines.

27. Criticism of specialised committees. The main points of criticism are as follows:

(*a*) they may lead to a narrowness of outlook;

(*b*) the existence of committees to examine estimates and to debate general policy would place too great a burden on ministers;

(*c*) they could weaken Parliament by linking it too closely with the executive and executive decisions;

(*d*) they present problems of staffing and support services.

28. The specialised committee experiment. The Labour Government in 1966–7 set up three specialised committees. Two were effectively attached to specific departments, i.e. Agriculture and Education and Science, and one cut across departmental lines, i.e. Science and Technology. In addition to the usual committee powers two new developments were introduced:

(*a*) they were empowered to examine witnesses in public;

(*b*) the Committee on Science and Technology had power to "appoint persons with technical or scientific knowledge for the purpose of public inquiries".

NOTE: Each committee was dissolved after only one session. The existence of specialist committees was further raised in 1970–1, through the establishment of the public expenditure committee, which has sub-committees covering particular groups of departments. The Government decided that specialist committees would continue to investigate areas of policy, though not attached to particular departments, e.g. race relations, Scottish affairs, and science and technology.

29. Achievements of the specialised committees. The main achievements of these committees were as follows.

(*a*) They secured co-operation from ministers in their capacity as responsible managers rather than as mere political figures.

(*b*) They established the habit of regular meetings away from Westminster.

(*c*) Ministers generally adopted a very free approach in giving evidence to the committees.

30. Disadvantages of the committees. These were as follows.

(*a*) There was a feeling that they tended to "type-cast" M.P.s.

(*b*) There was no simple set of tests which could be applied to available information to determine whether it was suitable for consideration by both the legislature and the executive, without the danger of inhibiting the process of policy-making.

31. Problems of specialist committees and executive control. In order to be successful the proper position of the committees in the constitutional set-up must be clearly established. This involves the following.

(*a*) *Role of committees.* Choice must be exercised as to the basic nature of such committees, namely whether they are to be:

   (*i*) objective, fact-finding committees;

   (*ii*) partisan, supporting committees;

   (*iii*) ministerial advisory committees.

(*b*) *The position of committees.* In order that such committees may be successful, and in particular those of the objective, fact-finding nature (which is the role generally established), it is necessary that:

   (*i*) a distinction be drawn between valuable division into party and non-party issues, instead of the largely unworkable policy and administration distinction;

   (*ii*) they must be sufficiently freed from the party whip control to sustain their objectivity.

(*c*) *Problems to be overcome.* They must answer the questions which faced the specialist committees during the experimental session of 1966–7.

   (*i*) How far can a specialist committee extend its inquiries beyond how money was spent, into what choice there had been in the use of real resources?

   (*ii*) How far could a specialist committee proceed from securing elucidation to influencing the course of decision-making?

32. Other forms of control.

(*a*) Public opinion and pressure groups (*see* XV).

(b) Judicial control (see XIV).
(c) Treasury control (see VIII).
(d) Cabinet control (see VI).

PROGRESS TEST 2

1. Outline some of the characteristics of the British system of government. **(1)**

2. Consider the meaning and application of the doctrine of the separation of powers. **(2–3)**

3. Why does the government dominate Parliament? **(4–6)**

4. Consider the position of the Cabinet and the Prime Minister in the British system of government. **(7–10)**

5. Examine the reasons for the existence of conventions. To what factors may obedience to conventions be attributed? **(11–14)**

6. Consider the contemporary role of Parliament. **(21)**

7. What criticisms may be made of the parliamentary committee system, and state how specialist committees might overcome such difficulties. **(25–27)**

8. Examine the experience of the use of specialised select committees. **(28–31)**

CHAPTER III

Organisational Theory

INTRODUCTION

1. Background. Owing to similarities between large-scale organisations it is possible to apply, with certain qualifications, the results of the study of private business to public organisations. The inter-relationship between private and public organisations has been emphasised in recent years both in terms of organisational characteristics and objectives. Factors contributing to this closer affinity include principally the following.

(*a*) The Second World War led to the introduction of non-career civil servants into Whitehall. Although these were generally only temporary attachments, when they returned to their former occupations, often in the private sector, their experiences provided a mutual interchange of ideas between the two sectors.

(*b*) The practice in recent years of making short-term civil service appointments from private sector managers.

(*c*) Nationalisation has had the effect of bringing private administrative structures within the public sector.

(*d*) The growth in the public sector of professions which operate in both the public and private sectors, e.g. in the field of management techniques.

2. Constraints. The qualifications which must be allowed for in such an approach and which therefore provide constraints in the application of such studies to public administration, are as follows.

(*a*) The nature of the basic administrative problem which varies substantially from the basic problem in private business. This problem has two basic elements:

(*i*) administration must accord with the social and economic environment;

(*ii*) it must provide that environment with services needed by society if it is to function and progress.

(b) In particular government disposes of coercive powers which do not arise in the private sector, and, partly for this reason, administrative decision-making is bound by rules of consultation, objection and appeal, which have no parallel in the private sector.

(c) Government undertakes or sponsors speculative ventures, e.g. in technology, which have no close equivalents.

(d) Whilst businessmen are strongly oriented to market innovation, public administration can be said to be concerned more with market compression, i.e. with the limitation of competing demands all of which cannot be met.

(e) The greater emphasis in public administration on law and the legal context within which such administration must function.

(f) The greater relationship in public administration with public welfare and its consequent organisational and operational ramifications.

(g) The responsibility of the public administrator to the public, a situation not matched in private industry.

(h) The difficulties of quantifying the goals of public administration in the absence of reliance on a pure profits test.

(i) The different considerations in determining goals in public administration, which are much wider than those in private industry.

NOTE: It must therefore always be borne in mind that public administration alone operates in a "political" framework, both in the sense of political responsibility and control, and in the sense that its objectives are based on different and wider criteria.

3. Objectives of public administration theory.

(a) Understanding organisational problems as they relate to the structure of public departments, their inter-relationships, co-ordination, and internal functioning.

(b) Understanding how people in organisations behave and how organisations function.

4. Problems of administrative functioning.
Gaps between administrative functioning and the demands of society may arise for a variety of reasons:

(a) the slow reaction of administration to changes in society;

(b) the loss of the faculty of initiative by administrators (*see* VII).

(*c*) the absence of coherence in action, which may be due to the overlapping of departmental functions, problems of co-ordination, and team-work;

(*d*) the imprecise and often obscure allocation of decision-making responsibilities, which involves difficulties in adapting to both individual and changing circumstances, as well as raising fundamental questions of competence.

5. Common organisational defects. Deficiencies common to all types of organisation include:

(*a*) unsatisfactory means of pursuit of objectives;

(*b*) failure of departments and sections within organisations to contribute to overall objectives at full cost value;

(*c*) lack of functional co-ordinative machinery;

(*d*) lack of co-ordination of inter-departmental activity;

(*e*) slow and poor quality decisions as a result of:

(*i*) overloading of managers;

(*ii*) inadequate information;

(*iii*) tendency to make decisions at an inappropriate level.

These problems thus necessitate solutions aimed at directing organisational activities and behaviour in the pursuit of organisational objectives, rationalising the intra-organisational structure to achieve full cost-value, providing machinery for co-ordination of functions and departments, and improving decision-making by provision of adequate information systems and satisfactory delegation principles.

ORGANISATION THEORY

6. Warning. In considering management theory and its application it is important to bear the following points in mind.

(*a*) Organisation theory does not exist as a coherent and universally accepted set of concepts.

(*b*) Organisation theory is not traditionally concerned with public administration. It is thus necessary when applying such theory to public administration to bear in mind that whilst organisational features may be similar, public administration operates in a much different institutional setting.

7. Approaches to organisation theory. Three broad approaches to organisation theory may be discerned.

(*a*) *Classical approach*. This is concerned with the study of activities that have to be undertaken to achieve objectives, and the grouping of such activities to achieve efficient specialisation and co-ordination.

(*b*) *Human relations or behavioural approach*. This involves a study of motives and behaviour and the development of criteria to help design an organisation that stimulates members to co-operate in achieving the organisation's aims.

(*c*) *Systems approach*. This approach concentrates on decisions that need to be made to achieve objectives, and the organisation is thus designed to facilitate decision-making.

THE CLASSICAL APPROACH

8. Basic principles. The nature of the classical approach was epitomised in the Report of the President's Committee on Administrative Management (Washington, 1937) in which it was stated that "the foundations of effective management, in public affairs no less than in private, are well known. They have emerged universally wherever men have worked together for a common purpose . . . stated in simple terms, these canons of efficiency require the establishment of a responsible and effective chief executive as the centre of energy, direction and administrative management; the systematic organisation of all activities in the hands of qualified personnel under the direction of the chief executive, and to aid him in this, the establishment of appropriate managerial and staff agencies".

9. Elements of the approach. The following are brief statements of the main features of the classical approach to organisations.

10. Determining objectives. The basic purpose of determining organisational objectives is seen as being to:

(*a*) establish management priorities;
(*b*) indicate key departments and activities;
(*c*) to avoid the "decibel" system of management;
(*d*) provide consistency of human and materials organisation with the objectives.

11. Specialisation and grouping. Classical theory treats specialisation as the basis of efficiency, and consequently places emphasis on the most effective management grouping of specialist functions.

12. Grouping. The approach identifies four relevant factors in grouping.

(*a*) *Span of control*. The classicists considered that one manager is only capable of controlling a limited number of subordinates. This view may be represented by the general approach of those such as Gulick ("where work is diversified, qualitative and . . . scattered, one man can supervise only a few") or the more specific approaches of those such as Graciunas, who claims specific practical maxima, e.g. three to six being representative.

(*b*) *Economies of scale*. Grouping should be achieved to produce economies of scale both from the technical and resource aspects, and from the management aspects.

(*c*) *Co-ordination*. Grouping may be justified and should be operated to achieve advantages of co-ordination. Co-ordination results in integration of individual effort, and weak co-ordination results in lack of "goal" consistency, uneconomical organisation, and poor specification of duties.

(*d*) *Grouping by nature of activity*. Key activities may be grouped under higher management for direct supervision. Such "key-ness" may result from the long-term nature of an activity, its important qualitative function or the repercussions its failure would have on other aspects of the organisation. The essence of such grouping is thus to place highly interdependent units under a unified head.

13. Delegation. Delegation has been defined as "the institutionalised right to make decisions or give orders on behalf of an organisation" (J. O'Shaughnessy, *Business Organisation*, Allen and Unwin, 1972). In the classical approach it was felt that delegation should be to the point closest to that of operation. Factors relevant to delegation include the following.

(*a*) Delegation makes possible the achievement of economies of scale and specialisation.

(*b*) Key activity decision-making is likely to evolve upwards to higher management.

(*c*) It diffuses the authority to make decisions to lower levels of the organisation thus enhancing initiative and job satisfaction as well as identification with the goals of the organisation.

(*d*) The view of the classicists was that authority should be delegated to the extent and in the way necessary for the accomplishment of the results expected. Therefore the extent of delegation should be matched by the particular job to be done.

14. Divisionalisation and decentralisation. Divisionalisation consists of dividing the organisation into units based on such factors as product type, geographical operation, etc. Decentralisation consists of the systematic delegation of authority to all organisational units. Centralisation, on the other hand, is the tendency to withhold such authority.

In practice, complete decentralisation is impossible, as central organisation must retain at least a minimum of power necessary to achieve the following:

(a) approve divisional objectives and ensure that these are compatible with the overall organisational objectives;

(b) approve the divisional organisational structure by indicating key departments.

15. Advantages and disadvantages of decentralisation. The advantages of decentralisation are as follows:

(a) it focuses efforts directly on performance and results;

(b) poor results do not remain hidden;

(c) management by objectives becomes fully effective;

(d) managers have the incentive of independent command;

(e) economies of scale, co-ordination, etc., are achieved.

The disadvantages are:

(f) the danger of over-independence from overall objectives;

(g) some delay in decision-making;

(h) the possibility of poor co-ordination at local level.

16. Essential conditions for effective decentralisation. The following points should be noted.

(a) There must be both strong parts and a strong centre.

(b) Decentralised units must be strong enough to support the standards of management required.

(c) Each federally decentralised unit should have growth potential.

(d) There must be enough scope and challenge in the managerial posts.

(e) Federal units should exist side by side.

17. Specifying responsibility. "Authority is not to be conceived of apart from responsibility which goes with the exercise of power. Responsibility is a corollary of authority; it is its natural consequence and essential counterpart, and wheresoever authority is exercised, responsibility arises." (Fayol, H, *General and Industrial Management,* Pitman, 1967.) The classical approach thus emphasised the need for clear specification of responsibility for the following reasons.

(*a*) Vague assignment of responsibility results in confusion and jurisdictional conflict.

(*b*) Accountability without specification of responsibility is inequitable.

(*c*) This permits the anticipation of future needs and the making of comparisons.

(*d*) It limits interference by supervisors.

18. Line and staff relations. Classical theory emphasised the establishment of line relationships, i.e. between superior and subordinates, for the following reasons.

(*a*) It establishes official lines of communication throughout the organisation.

(*b*) It establishes to whom each subordinate is accountable.

(*c*) It establishes responsibility for co-ordination of the functions of subordinates.

Line services are thus conceived of as vertical relationships, and staff services as horizontal supporting activities. The former are thus direct contributors to the organisation's objectives, whereas staff units provide the necessary adjectival services to the line functions and thus contribute indirectly to the overall organisational objectives, e.g. personnel, finance, purchasing. In classical theory, line is equated with command and staff with advice.

19. Conflicts in the theory. The following points should be noted.

(*a*) Line members frequently resent control exercised by staff.

(*b*) Staff personnel are generally new additions to an organisation, and therefore uncertain as to their status. This gives rise to relationship difficulties, namely:

　　(*i*) difficulty in quantifying staff functions;

(*ii*) the indirect nature of staff functions;

(*iii*) the possibility that staff may push line too hard in order to justify their existence;

(*iv*) a tendency to appear superior on the part of the staff;

(*v*) the possibility that staff may adopt an "ivory tower" approach.

20. Improving relations. These difficulties may to some extent be resolved by the following measures.

(*a*) Specify responsibility clearly.

(*b*) Encourage each to become better acquainted with the other's work.

(*c*) Rotate staff and line assignments.

(*d*) Establish an "overall management climate".

21. Major defects in classical theory. In broad terms the approach has been criticised by A. K. Rice (*The Enterprise and Its Environment: A System Theory of Management Organisation*, Tavistock Publications, 1963) as being based on a "closed system with an inherent ability to accommodate changes in the external environment". In particular the following major criticisms may be made.

(*a*) *Underlying assumptions.* The basic classical assumptions have been challenged in that they oversimplify, and fail to take account of the development of small informal groups and sub-groups which may be at odds with the overall organisation goals.

(*b*) *Problem definition.* Problems arise, in public administration, particularly where objectives are difficult to define or where various activities are unquantifiable, e.g. where social criteria are involved. The classical approach presumes both the importance and the ease of defining objectives and fails to recognise that in public administration the definition of such objectives is interwoven with the broad political process.

(*c*) *Means not ends.* The approach concentrates on the means whereby objectives may be achieved, but gives little or no guide to the relevant elements in establishing such ends. Consequently the approach is unrelated to the social and political problems faced by members of an organisation.

THE HUMAN RELATIONS APPROACH

22. Principles. The human relations or behavioural approach is principally concerned with designing a social environment within an organisation that stimulates individuals to strive to achieve the overall organisational objectives. The organisation it thus seeks to achieve should:

(*a*) both achieve its objectives and satisfy members;

(*b*) encourage high productivity and low absenteeism;

(*c*) stimulate co-operation and avoid destructive conflicts.

NOTE: Its principal objection to the classical approach is that the latter ignores people's likely behaviour under different organisational arrangements.

23. Practice. In practice, the approach is concerned with the following.

(*a*) *Needs and wants.* The approach involves the study of an individual's wants and needs, factors stimulating these and goals which satisfy such needs. Needs have been classified as physical, safety, social, egoistic, and self-actualisation (Argyris, C., *Personality and Organisation*, Hooper & Row, 1972). The classical concentration on specialisation, span of control, etc., is rejected as being inconsistent with needs and wants.

(*b*) *Work groups.* The approach recognises the influence which associates of an individual have on the individual's attitudes and behaviour. It points out that an individual does not operate in isolation and in particular:

(*ii*) he tends to conform to group pressures;

(*ii*) his attitudes and morale are influenced by group associations;

(*iii*) problem-solving and leadership are often group functions.

(*c*) *Supervisory behaviour.* This is treated as a vital factor in influencing work group behaviour, as the supervisor represents the link between the group and the formal organisation.

24. Criticism of group participation. Group participation in decision-making has been criticised for the following reasons:

(*a*) group participation increases group domination of its members;

(*b*) responsibilities become blurred;

(*c*) group and expert judgments may conflict;

(*d*) the cost of re-orientating supervisory functions may exceed the benefits of group participation;

(*e*) the process is not automatically effective and depends greatly on supervisory and management attitudes.

NOTE: The approach is also vitally concerned with inter-group behaviour and study of relations between groups rather than between individuals. Such behaviour is an important factor in achieving objectives, and in assessing the degree of co-operation and co-ordination required.

25. Conclusions. The classical and human relations approaches thus vary in the following important respects.

(*a*) Whereas the human relations school is concerned with the organisation evolving effectively from inter-personal behaviour, the classical approach pre-determines the organisation within which individuals are required to function.

(*b*) The human relations approach results in a comparatively flat organisational structure, whereas the classical approach results in a pyramidal structure as, for example, in the British civil service.

(*c*) Authority is regarded by the human relations approach as a social factor, by the classicists as organisational.

(*d*) Interdependence is a key factor in the human relations approach, which considers that the classical definition of responsibility creates competition.

THE SYSTEMS APPROACH

26. Principles. The systems approach treats an organisation as an example of a "system", i.e. a set of interdependent parts forming a whole with the objective of fulfilling some definable function. A business organisation is essentially regarded as a decision-making system, and the organisation is treated as being built up from an analysis of information requirements and communications networks. It thus treats the process of decision-making as basic to the determination of objectives and policies.

27. Scope. The methodology of the systems approach thus consists of the following steps:

(*a*) specifying objectives;
(*b*) establishing sub-systems (main decision areas);
(*c*) analysing these decision areas and their information needs;
(*d*) designing the communication channels to facilitate information flow within the organisation;
(*e*) grouping decision areas to minimise communication problems. In practice the approach illustrates the importance of organisation of information, the advantages of project rather than functional division and the need to centrally concentrate the information network.

28. A contemporary outlook. The contemporary approach to the theory of organisations is to abandon the idea of treating organisations as mere passive instruments operating in response to external pressures. Organisations are regarded as semi-autonomous systems which develop their own internal goals, e.g. Simon refers to their having "performance objectives" and "conservation objectives", the latter relating to the organisation's desire to survive.

Argyris defines an organisation as "an organic inter-relation of parts" which has essentially three activities, namely:

(*a*) achieving particular objectives;
(*b*) maintaining itself internally;
(*c*) adapting to the internal environment.

DECISION-MAKING

29. The decision-making process in management. The rational comprehensive approach deals with decision-making as a programme of logical and sequential steps, namely:

(*a*) recognition and diagnosis of problem;
(*b*) determination of alternative solutions;
(*c*) investigation and analysis of facts relating to each alternative;
(*d*) comparison of the consequences of the alternatives;
(*e*) selection of solution.

Decision-making is essentially *complex*. A decision is not the province of any single individual, but the result of contributions of knowledge from both inside and outside the organisation being integrated, even though the final direction might emanate from a single person or group of individuals.

30. Advantages of process.

(a) It can be used to clarify the general logic of a problem and to accustom decision-makers to look out for aspects of the problem which are capable of quantification.

(b) It can be simulated under laboratory conditions to ascertain the effects of different incentives, working conditions, and social factors on the speed and accuracy of possible solutions.

31. Limitations. The approach is however an essentially static process and is subject to the following limitations.

(a) Values to be realised are not usually set out clearly and distinctly.

(b) Implicit objectives emerge during the decision-making process itself which may conflict with the originally perceived objectives.

(c) It is generally difficult for the individual decision-maker to take a comprehensive view of the whole problem, as the solution is invariably a lengthy and cumulative process.

(d) Most organisations would be paralysed if the process was carried out completely in all cases. Because of the need for speed decisions will often necessarily have to be taken on the basis of incomplete data.

32. Behavioural approach. This attempts to examine how people make decisions under conditions of imperfect information. It seeks to show as a *dynamic* process how decisions are affected by individual differences, social pressures, leadership styles, and communication structures.

It suffers however from certain methodological problems, in particular:

(a) confidentiality in decision-making will often necessitate research being carried out under simulated conditions;

(b) there are considerable difficulties in isolating the actual decision under consideration from the stream of consultations, committee deliberations, etc.

However, the approach provides a framework descriptive of the decision-making process.

33. Framework for decision-making. A decision is seen as being reached in the following stages:

(a) *awareness* of the existence of the problem, e.g. through political channels, interest group consultation, internal research and information;

(b) the problem is then *structured*, i.e. it is interpreted and related to other information so that the nature of the problem is clarified;

(c) *exploration*, where possible courses of action or inaction are listed and an estimate of the consequences made;

(d) *evaluation* and provisional decision;

(e) *consultation*;

(f) *authorisation* by higher level authority.

34. Bounded rationality. There is a need with complex problems which are beyond the competence of a single decision maker to resort to factorisation. This division may be on a horizontal, or, more typically in public administration, on a vertical basis. The vertical approach is a reflection of hierarchical structure, i.e. the typical Weberian Bureaucracy (*see* VII). In such cases the basic structural problem is to bring together the independent factors involved, and in this respect an organisation can be perceived as a system of communication. As such it involves the allocation of duties in such a way as to allow individuals to contribute rationally to the solution of complex problems, but however rational the structure it is *bounded* by the competence of its members.

35. Organisational restraints in decision-making. The internal restraints of an organisation may prevent the following of the ideal process. Research has shown that an organisation contains certain norms which inhibit the open confrontation of certain issues, and which generate a resistance or feeling of resistance to change. These are as follows:

(a) social constraints;

(b) leadership style;

(c) outside pressures such as impossibility of separating administration and politics;

(d) a tendency in bureaucratic organisations to concentrate on "sunk costs";

(e) outside reference groups.

36. Common errors in decision-making. The most common errors are as follows.

(*a*) *Cognitive nearsightedness*. This is the tendency to make decisions satisfy immediate needs. This is particularly attractive in intra-government business, with expediency being the key factor, e.g. the overcrowding of Negroes in some cities in the U.S.A. was expedient to solve the housing shortage but has unfortunate long-term affects which were not considered.

(*b*) *Over-simplification*. The tendency to deal with symptoms to the exclusion of causes.

(*c*) *Over-reliance on personal experience*.

(*d*) *Pre-conceived notions*. These lead to ignoring of social science findings if they contradict the ideas of the decision-makers. This has been particularly noticeable in British economic policy-making (*see* VII).

BEHAVIOUR IN ORGANISATIONS

37. Importance of behavioural studies. Public administration studies often tend to concentrate on the machinery of administration, to the exclusion of those factors influencing behaviour in organisations, and consequently influencing an organisation's effectiveness. Any public administration system depends for its effectiveness on both organisational factors and behaviour within that structure.

38. Preliminary factors. The following points should be noted.

(*a*) *Conscious and unconscious behaviour*. It is necessary, in order to obtain an overall picture of the way an individual functions in an organisation, to study both the easily recognisable conscious choices which he brings to bear on his role, and also those unconscious choices which are largely conditioned by habits, experience, skills, etc., previously acquired by the individual.

(*b*) *Behavioural premises*. These have been defined as "the criteria or guides used in narrowing down the multitude of possibilities to a single actuality" (H. A. Simon, D. W. Smithburg and V. A. Thomson, *Public Administration*, Alfred A. Knopf, 1967). Such underlying premises will involve both value and factual elements. The former correspond to the "ends" of behaviour and are involved in the definition of objectives, whereas the latter correspond to the "means" by which the objective is to be achieved.

NOTE: Value elements may themselves contain factual elements in that they in themselves represent means to further ends.

(c) *Rational and irrational behaviour*. Although the primary concern of public administration study is the achievement of goals by rational means, it is a mistake to ignore irrational behaviour. Irrational behaviour, when studied, may reveal matters which may distort or explain deviations from otherwise rational objectives.

39. Value premises. These may be understood as factors influencing behaviour apparent in organisational structures. They principally include the following.

(a) *The organisation's objectives*. The organisation's objectives expressed as objects of activities, groups to be served, level or quality of service, etc., enter into every administration system.

(b) *Efficiency*. Examined pragmatically public administration is concerned with the efficient utilisation of resources, as are other organisations.

This premise operates towards the adoption of methods of achieving objectives which will involve lower costs or, where appropriate, will provide the greater results.

NOTE: In public administration measurement of efficiency becomes a major problem as pure economic results must often be set against social objectives, etc. This does not, however, invalidate the value premise of efficiency but merely requires different standards of measurement, e.g. management by objectives.

(c) *Individual rights*. In organisations involving regular contact with individuals and social problems, an underlying premise of "fair play" may operate. This premise will be devalued in organisations where the structure approaches a pure bureaucratic model (*see* VII), as the members will be trained or the rules framed to minimise personal factors.

(d) *Personal values*. These are "non-organisational" values and arise where individuals tend to evaluate the organisation's objectives in terms of their own personal objectives. The success of an organisation may well depend on the degree to which it is able to replace such personal values with the organisation's objectives.

40. Organisation and non-organisation objectives. When personal values conflict with the goals of the organisation it will be necessary for the organisation to offer such incentives as will effectively subjugate the personal values of individuals to those of the organisation. Incentives may be defined as the appeals an organisation makes to the personal values of its employees to induce them to accept organisational values in choice and decision-making. Incentives have been classified by Chester Barnard as follows:

(a) material inducement:
(b) opportunities for distinction;
(c) good physical working conditions;
(d) personal confidence and satisfaction in social relationships within the organisation;
(e) conformity with habitual practices;
(f) feeling of participation.

41. Factual premises. These are difficult to tabulate, but in general terms include those factors resulting in the acquisition of skills and knowledge to deal with information.

42. Organisational influences on behavioural premises. The two principal organisational influences are as follows:

(a) influences brought to bear on individuals through the formal organisational process;
(b) influences brought to bear by informal organisations, i.e. by informal social structures and relations which develop within a formal organisation.

43. Extra-organisational influences on behavioural premises. These may in general terms be regarded as conditioning that the individual receives before he becomes a member of the organisation, and influences to which he is subjected whilst a member of the organisation but which do not stem from the organisation itself, e.g. personal factors, family and social influences. The principal extra-organisational influences are as follows.

(a) *Community mores*. This involves the behavioural attitudes and beliefs held by the community in which the individual lives. They will include established patterns which are enforced throughout society in the form of social customs, obligations, standards, etc., and will affect the individual's attitudes towards such matters as authority, status and efficiency as business and personal concepts.

(b) *Personality factors*. Although this is primarily a subject of psychological study it is worth observing that individual differences in personality will exist as a result of varying heredity and environmental factors. In the context of administrative organisations these will manifest themselves in an individual's attitudes to objectivity, sociability, ambition, etc.

(c) *Outside organisations*. The behavioural patterns and objectives established by the organisation in which the individual operates may be subject to opposing standards and patterns of behaviour set by organisations to which an individual belongs or is influenced by outside the work context, e.g. church, political organisations, etc.

(d) *Prior training*. This may influence attitudes taken by individuals towards various organisation objectives or means of achieving objectives. A particularly good example is the antipathy of the civil service administrative class towards professionalism.

44. The influence of formal and informal organisations. An organisational setting will result in an individual acting differently than he would do in a non-organisational context, or if he was in a different organisational setting. There is thus an assumption of an organisational role, i.e. an organisationally and socially defined standardised pattern of behaviour. In consequence behaviour is affected by the following:

(a) assumption of the organisation's objectives;

(b) acceptance of the influence of informal organisations within the organisation;

(c) expectations;

(d) organisational morale.

45. "Administrative man." As a result of such influences, an individual becomes what has been described as "administrative man" by Simon: "He accepts the organisation's goals as the value premises of his decisions, is particularly sensitive and reactive to the influences upon him by other members of his organisation, forms stable expectations regarding his own role in relation to others and the roles of others in relation to him, and has a high morale in regard to the organisation goals" (H. A. Simon, D. W. Smithburg and V. A. Thomson, *Public Administration*, Alfred Knopf, 1967).

46. Formal and informal differences. In formal organisations patterns of behaviour and relations are deliberately and legitimately planned for members of the organisation, i.e. the division of work and allocation of responsibilities, authority relationships, etc., are established. In informal organisations the actual pattern of behaviour and relations of members of an organisation will depart to differing extents from the formal organisational plan. This difference may arise through the need to supplement an incomplete formal organisation or to reduce conflicts therein. In consequence, an individual's behaviour will be a result of both formal and informal organisational influences.

PROGRESS TEST 3

1. What constraints restrict the use of organisation theory in public administration? **(2)**

2. Outline the main groups of organisation theory. **(7, 8, 22, 26)**

3. Explain the meaning and importance of (a) grouping, and (b) specialisation. **(12, 13)**

4. What are the main defects of classical organisation theory? **(21)**

5. Distinguish the classical and human relations approaches. **(25)**

6. What are the advantages and difficulties in the rational comprehensive method of decision making? **(29–31)**

7. What are meant by "value premises"? **(39)**

8. How do organisations influence value premises? **(42, 44)**

9. What are the main extra-organisational influences on behaviour? **(43)**

CHAPTER IV

Central Administration
I: Machinery

FEATURES

1. Introduction. There are few discernible trends underlying the principles upon which British central government departments have been developed. Basic patterns which have emerged, however, include the following.

(*a*) *Functional principle.* In general terms, the basic allocation of responsibilities has developed on a functional basis.

(*b*) *Absence of uninterrupted development.* With the principal exceptions of the Treasury and the Foreign and Home Offices the majority of government departments have incurred functional reorganisation since the nineteenth century, in consequence of which it is impossible to portray an uninterrupted development of the central government machine.

(*c*) *Continual process.* The process of development is best viewed as one of continuous fusion and fission (*see* **4** (*b*) and (*c*)).

(*d*) *Integration.* The trend in the early 1970s in departmental organisation was towards integration as the best means of achieving co-ordination and policy formulation and execution. This was typified by the reorganisation of the Department of the Environment and the Department of Trade and Industry, though the Department of Trade and Industry was subsequently dismantled by the Labour Government in 1974 into four separate departments, and the Department of Transport was hived off from the Department of the Environment, both due to management difficulties in organising and co-ordinating "super-departments".

2. The continuous process. The continuous and changing pattern and bases of development of the central departments is due to a number of factors, in particular the following:

(a) expansion of the scope and nature of government activity;

(b) development of new areas of policy, e.g. the social services;

(c) fluctuations in the degree of emphasis accorded to different fields of administration;

(d) party political factors, i.e. the tendency to create a department for a minister rather than vice versa.

3. The system of departments. Although in the British system the major organisational unit is the Ministry or Department, these vary in a number of important respects.

(a) *Policy administration*. Although most departments have some degree of responsibility for subordinate organisations distinctions may be drawn between departments which are responsible for the direct administration of policy, e.g. the Treasury, and those charged with formulating policy as a basis for the control of other agencies, e.g. the Department of the Environment with its overall responsibility for local government. However, certain departments cut across this division e.g. the Department of Trade and Industry (D.T.I.) which whilst having been responsible for executing policy in relation to commerce and industry was also responsible for administering policy in relation to various public corporations. However, from its inception, the D.T.I. had management problems. It was a huge department and, although its responsibilities had a common basis in being related to trade and industry, it was more like a conglomerate than a really close-knit integrated department. The break-up of the D.T.I. was completed by the Labour Government in March 1974, and its work split between four departments, each headed by a Secretary of State with cabinet status, i.e. Energy, Prices and Consumer Protection, Industry, and Trade.

(b) *Executive or service*. The former type of department is primarily concerned with the execution of services authorised by Parliament, whereas the latter is concerned with the provision of common services for the administration itself. With the absorption of the Ministry of Works which was the most important service department, and with the growing tendency of departments to operate their own manpower and accounting functions this distinction is now less valid, but does still include such as the H.M.S.O., which, like the Central Office of Information, is an agency without a political head.

(c) *Geographical coverage*. Various departments can be

considered in geographical terms, e.g. the Foreign Office and the Board of Customs and Excise.

(d) *Centralised and decentralised*. A distinction may be drawn on the basis of contact with members of the public, as opposed to contact with representative interests of the public. Examples in this category may be drawn from the Department of Employment, the Department of Health and Social Security, and the Inland Revenue.

However, the above represents a descriptive approach and as such does not attempt to provide a formula for the allocation of responsibilities (*see* 4), nor guidance as to the major problems of control and co-ordination (*see* 15–26).

ALLOCATION OF FUNCTIONS

4. Theory of allocation. The following means of allocation should be noted.

(a) *By function*. The creation of departments to administer particular functions of government is generally regarded as offering the best chance of achieving efficiency despite the frequent difficulty of deciding exact criteria for such allocation. In particular, if operated with reasonable accuracy, it should avoid excessive duplication and overlapping of functions and will encourage the acquisition of special skills and knowledge. Additionally it allows a complex of matters to be studied as a whole, and enables a clarity of decision-making responsibility to emerge to the consequent benefit of the public.

However, it cannot entirely eliminate overlapping, it is not always appropriate and in certain cases there is a demonstrable need for a clientele or regional basis.

(b) *By clientele*. The creation of departments related not to function but to clientele is only suitable where a group is so special that its problems are incapable of being related to those of the nation as a whole.

"The inevitable outcome of this method of organisation is a tendency to Lilliputian administration. It is impossible that the specialised service which each department has to render to the community can be of as high a standard when its work is at the same time limited to a particular class of persons and extended to every variety of provision for them, as when the Department concentrates itself on the provision of one particular service only by whomsoever required and looks beyond the interests of comparatively small classes" (Haldane Committee, 1918).

(c) *By process employed*. Advocates of allocation according to "work process" claim that this results in the highest possible degree of technical specialisation. The main objection to such an allocation is that departments would require a high degree of subsequent co-ordination in order to execute policy, whilst at the same time making such co-ordination difficult. This would result from the impossibility of achieving any one complete administrative process from any department, and would necessitate co-operation to achieve execution of policy from a number of other departments each staffed by probably antagonistic experts.

(d) *Regional principle*. Despite its application in certain limited circumstances, e.g. Scottish and Welsh Offices, this method of allocation poses the problem of assimilating regional matters to those of the nation as a whole. Particularly is this the case in national economic and physical planning. Regional interests are probably best dealt with by regional decentralisation (*see* XI).

5. Underlying distributional criteria.

(a) The location of any governmental service or activity may depend on the policy of the government within a particular field rather than on any theoretical basis of allocation, e.g. defence procurements were transferred from the Ministry of Aviation to the Ministry of Technology in 1967 and then to a sub-group in 1970, viz. the Ministry of Aviation Supply. In 1971 the Ministry of Aviation Supply was abolished and its functions split between the Ministry of Defence and the Department of Trade and Industry. In 1978 the responsibility lay solely with the Ministry of Defence. As has been commented "the great changes in administration have come about through causes partly fortuitous, partly political, but on the whole outside the range of administrative planning" (MacKenzie).

(b) Trends towards the development of super-ministries may be explained on the grounds of political desire to keep the size of the Cabinet to manageable levels, and by a preference for co-ordination of different functions within a single ministry rather than face the problem of inter-departmental co-ordination. The

Labour Government which took office in 1974 reversed markedly the trend towards super departments, in particular it split the Department of Trade into four Ministries in 1974, and re-established the Department of Transport in 1976.

(c) Though this should not be overstated there is consideration of the force of individual political personalities in determining administrative structure.

6. The process of departmental creation. It is now appropriate to relate theories of allocation, etc., to the pattern of development in British central departments. Although the pattern assumed has varied between different services and over different periods, four main concepts have emerged as follows.

(a) Separate departments will be developed where individual or grouped functions become sufficiently important or complex, or involve other administrative problems which necessitate the creation of a single department for their resolution.

(b) The process of fusion may occur, which involves gathering together related services into a single department, the object being to ensure coherent development and co-ordination of such functions, e.g. the 1970 government reorganisation (*see* **7–10**).

(c) The process of fission involves the division of responsibilities between departments which have previously been concentrated in a single organisation. It will generally occur where the diseconomies of concentration exceed the economies of scale and lead to the growth of unwieldy masses with accompanying administrative inertia, e.g. the division of the old Ministry of Health into Health, Housing and Local Government, and Social Security.

(d) Although the transfer of functions is an automatic adjunct to the processes of fusion and fission, the converse is not the case, and may result in the transfer of functions between two or more existing departments. This has been described by Appleby as having "the object of producing coherent missions" (quoted in Hanson, A. M. and Walles, M., *Governing Britain*, Fontana, 1970).

NOTE: The interaction of political and administrative factors often accompanies the transfer process, and thus administrative convenience, though being the pragmatic motive for transfer, is not the sole criterion.

WHITE PAPER, 1970

7. Reorganisation of government. The White Paper (Cmnd. 4506, 1970) had the following underlying policies:

(*a*) the improvement of the quality of policy formulation and decision-making;

(*b*) the improvement of the framework in which public policy is formulated by "matching the field of responsibility of government departments to coherent fields of policy and administration" and "ensuring that the government machine responds and adapts to new policies within the broad framework of the main departmental fields of responsibility".

In order to translate these broad aims into organisational principles, changes were necessitated both in the methods of operation between departments and in departmental organisation itself.

8. Functional approach. The White Paper recommended that government departments should be functionally based for the following reasons:

(*a*) the purpose of organisation is to serve policy;

(*b*) related policy issues should be grouped in organisational terms;

(*c*) lines of demarcation are clarified by such groupings and overlapping is minimised;

(*d*) economies of scale are achieved;

(*e*) diffusion of expert knowledge is avoided, and co-ordination difficulties reduced.

NOTE: The White Paper contained the proviso that functional organisation does not always invalidate other allocations, but should provide a basis for allocation within non-functionally organised departments, e.g. the Welsh and Scottish Offices.

9. Unification of functions. The grouping of functions into wide-span departments was considered to provide the best basis for a series of fields of unified policy, and offered the following advantages.

(*a*) *Single strategy*. Such departments would have the capacity to propose and carry through a single strategy for clearly defined and accepted objectives.

(*b*) *Resolving conflicts*. It would provide a basis for the resolution of executive decision and policy-forming conflicts within the line of management, rather than by inter-departmental compromise.

(*c*) *Management*. It enlarges a department's capacity to manage and co-ordinate large resource-consuming projects within departmental boundaries.

(*d*) *Delegation*. A more rational and effective delegation of executive tasks is facilitated.

(*e*) *Identification*. The enlarged comprehensive departments will have a more direct identification with the community.

(*f*) *Contribution to strategy*. A more effective contribution to the government's overall strategy will be possible.

10. Reservations. However, the following disadvantages operated.

(*a*) The advantages would have been reduced if issues which truly necessitate inter-departmental discussion were taken solely in the unified department, without collective ministerial participation and responsibility.

(*b*) Mere aggregation of functions into a series of large departments could have given rise to management problems due to the size and complexity of the top organisational structure. It was therefore necessary to clearly define the boundaries of the functional wings which made up a large department. It would also be necessary to ensure that blocks of executive work would be delegated to accountable units of management, thus lightening the load on top management.

11. Changes since 1973.

(*a*) *Department of Trade and Industry*. This was divided in 1974 into four separate departments, viz. the Departments of Industry, Trade, Prices and Consumer Protection, and Energy. This represents the major swing from the concept of super-departments but does pose problems of control and co-ordination which have to be resolved through machinery both at the policy-making and the administrative levels.

(*b*) *Foreign and Commonwealth Office*. Briefly traced over the period from 1952 governmental functions in this area have developed as follows.

(*i*) In 1965 the old Colonial Office and the Commonwealth

Relations Office were merged to form the Commonwealth Office.

(*ii*) In 1967 the Foreign Office and the Commonwealth Office were merged into the Foreign and Commonwealth Office.

(*iii*) In 1969 the Foreign and Commonwealth Office (including Overseas Development Administration) was established and took in the Ministry of Overseas Development (established in 1963 to take over responsibility for technical co-operation).

(*iv*) Finally in 1973 the Foreign and Commonwealth Office was split into the Foreign and Commonwealth Office and the Ministry of Overseas Development.

(*c*) *Department of the Environment*. In 1976 a separate Ministry of Transport Industries was created apart from the Department of the Environment, though the Department retained responsibility for common services. Therefore the functions of the Department of the Environment largely reverted to those of the former Ministry of Housing and Local Government but with the additional responsibility for the construction industry and oversight of the Property Services Agency.

(*d*) *Department of Energy*. In 1976 the responsibility for negotiations with the oil companies regarding North Sea Development was transferred to the Department of Energy from the nondepartmental Duchy of Lancaster.

CONCLUSIONS ON DISTRIBUTION

12. Distinguishable principles. The following points should be noted.

(*a*) The Haldane Committee (1918) made a general attempt to define criteria for functional distribution. It considered the choice to lie between functional and clientele bases and concluded strongly in favour of the functional method. The Committee's approach, however, was too general to be of any real value.

(*b*) No consistent pattern has been followed. "They are the product of specific attempts to remedy imbalances and incoherences, to place functions where they may be most effectively performed, to emphasise certain responsibilities of government at the expense of others and to give satisfaction to political demands whether emanating from party politicians or the public." (Hanson, A. M. and Walles, M., *Governing Britain*, Fontana, 1970.)

(c) Because of the incoherence of principles of development, emphasis has been placed on the problems of co-ordination and overall planning, rather than on those of demarcation.

13. Observations on the White Paper. The following points should be noted.

(a) It has been suggested that the reorganisation increases the power of the executive arm of government and consequently reduces its effective accountability to Parliament (*see* II).

(b) As the government grows stronger, its relative strength is increased by concentration of power in a diminishing number of hands.

(c) It is illustrative of the trend to co-ordination through integration.

(d) The innovation of the Central Policy Review Staff should be noted (*see* V, **16**).

14. Internal organisation. Before examining general features of such organisation it is important to bear in mind that whilst subscribing to the ideal of an internal organisation which fosters efficiency, such ideals must be seen in the light of other, and possibly conflicting, ideals, which will affect such structures, e.g. accountability to Parliament, Treasury control, and compatability with civil service procedures. Given these constraints it may be stated that a "typical" department will exhibit the following features.

(a) It will be headed by a *Minister* or *Secretary of State* who carrries the political responsibility to Parliament for the department's functioning. This will in turn have repercussions for structure and such structure will have to accommodate the constitutional convention of responsibility, the legal constraints upon the department's powers, and the scrutiny to which the department may be subjected.

(b) The head of the permanent administrative staff will be a *Permanent Secretary*. He is effectively the accounting officer of the department and the nature of his role effectively results in centralisation and hierarchy in organisational terms.

(c) The Minister's *Private Office* consisting of the personal secretariat of the Minister headed by a civil servant of principal rank. The function of the private office is to organise, in conjunction with his Parliamentary counterpart, the work for which the

Minister is responsible for on a day-to-day basis, e.g. the answering of parliamentary questions.

(*d*) Departments are then typically divided into *divisions* each responsible for the department's major responsibilities. Each division is headed by an *under-secretary* and further divided into *branches* headed by an *assistant secretary*. Branches are again sub-divided under the control of principals. Finally divisions will normally be grouped under a *deputy-secretary*.

(*e*) Departments tend structurally to reflect the structural divisions in the civil service ranking hierarchy, thus resulting in a hierarchical structure characterised by an excessive number of levels.

CO-ORDINATION OF CENTRAL GOVERNMENT

15. The problem of co-ordination. The absence of uniform principles of allocation has led to a relative increase in the study of methods of co-ordination. Such co-ordination may be grouped into the following.

(*a*) *Primary co-ordination*, which deals with the co-ordination of interdependent activities with a department or between departments carrying out related functions. Simon has defined the need for such co-ordination in the following terms: "group behaviour requires not only the adoption of correct decisions, but also the adoption by all members of a group of the same decision". He sees organisational authority as a "relation that serves by sub-ordinating the decisions of the individual to the communicated decisions of others". Within a department these may be seen as the functions of the equivalent of a "line manager" in industry, and at inter-departmental level through the medium of inter-departmental committees and the informal relations of civil servants.

(*b*) *Executive level*. This involves co-ordination through Treasury responsibility and control, and now through the co-ordinating functions of the Civil Service Department.

(*c*) At the *political level* co-ordination is carried out through the Cabinet, the Cabinet secretariat, and Cabinet committees.

NOTE: A further co-ordination problem occurs in devising means whereby external values may be inculcated in those working within the department in order to enable functions to be carried out in the light of the beliefs in which the State should exercise its functions. This will be manifested through indoctrination training, or more formally through financial controls, appeals system, and obligatory consultation procedures.

16. Problems arising from functional approach. A certain amount of friction is caused by this approach in the area of inter-departmental responsibilities. Such disputes are not generally amenable to Treasury co-ordination owing to the limited number of departments involved, and the often specialised nature of the problems. Such problems in practice may be resolved by the following.

(*a*) *Periodical reallocation of duties*. This will occur in order to concentrate decision-taking responsibility at a single point.

(*b*) *Informal elements*. The informal activities of senior civil servants.

(*c*) *Formal methods*. These will include the use of formal inter-departmental committees or conferences, though these are subject to certain disadvantages in that they are subject to a *liberum veto* of members, and may tend to achieve co-operation at the level of the lowest common denominator.

17. Control of policy execution. Simon distinguished procedural and substantive co-ordination in the following terms. "By procedural is meant the specification of the organisation itself—that is, the generalised description of the behaviours and relationships of the members of the organisation. Procedural co-ordination establishes the lines of authority and outlines the spheres of activity of each organisation member, while substantive co-ordination specifies the content of his work." These functions may be considered in the light of the work of the Treasury and the Civil Service Department.

18. Treasury control. Details of Treasury control are dealt with in detail in VIII, but its main functions in this area may be stated as follows:

(*a*) financial control for the purpose of *substantive co-ordination* to ensure that policy objectives are achieved;

(*b*) the rule that no legislation requiring expenditure may go before the House of Commons without the support of a Treasury minister;

(*c*) the maintenance of agreed procedures and methods of

working e.g. in relation to the form of departmental accounts and the method of the presentation of estimates (*procedural co-ordination*).

19. Civil Service Department. The Department's main area of concern lies in the standardisation and development of personnel and management functions within departments, as compared with the Treasury which is more concerned with overall manpower policy.

20. Co-ordination of policy-making. This entails co-ordination over the development of new policy, political strategies, and new methods of working through individual departmental constituents of the overall government machine.

21. The Cabinet's general role as co-ordinator. The Cabinet is effectively the centre of the administrative system and is the major instrument of government in Britain. Its central role takes three forms.

(*a*) *Constitutional*. The administration derives its authority from the Cabinet.

(*b*) *Hierarchical*. Cabinet decisions and the minutes in which they are recorded constitute the primary administrative documents.

(*c*) *Administrative*. Formally, at least, major decision-making originates in the Cabinet and initiates chain reactions (*see* V). In addition, the Cabinet exercises vital administrative functions in its role as co-ordinator, director, planner and supervisor.

NOTE: The political functions of the Cabinet necessarily colour all its relations with the administration.

22. Methods of co-ordination by the Cabinet. The Cabinet provides formal machinery for co-ordination in its role as "final court of administrative appeal" and, below Cabinet level, with the exception of the Treasury, co-ordination is largely informal. Devices which have been adopted by the Cabinet for the achievement of administrative co-ordination may be summarised as follows:

(*a*) *ad hoc* committees;
(*b*) standing committees;
(*c*) "overlords";

(*d*) creation of co-ordinating departments;

(*e*) amalgamation of departments into "super-departments" under a single head.

23. Cabinet committees. These are one of the major post-war developments in the field of government administration. They may be of an *ad hoc* nature, being constituted temporarily to deal with specific problems or, more commonly, be standing committees, permanently constituted, dealing with specific areas of government, e.g. social services, economic policy, etc. Originally it was the practice for senior non-departmental ministers to preside over such committees, though it is now more common for Cabinet ministers with departmental responsibilities to preside, e.g. 1978, the Chancellor of the Exchequer, presided over the Public Expenditure Scrutiny Committee, while Harold Wilson, when Prime Minister, presided over two or three Cabinet committees.

The committees are empowered to deal with particular inter-departmental matters and in many cases have the power to make binding decisions without recourse to the Cabinet.

24. "Overlords." The period 1951–55 saw the use of "overlords" as the primary co-ordinating agency, i.e. non-departmental ministers were responsible for the co-ordination of food and agricultural policy, and for transport, fuel and power.

The method was criticised for the following reasons:

(*a*) it detracted from the status of departmental ministers;

(*b*) it raised problems of ministerial responsibility;

(*c*) difficulty was occasioned in defining the actual role of "overlords"; i.e. whether they were to be directors or merely advisers and co-ordinators.

NOTE: The system of Cabinet committees (*see* **23**) enables effective co-ordination of departmental policies without recourse to "overlords" and their attendant problems.

25. Co-ordinating departments. Constitutionally it is a logical progression from the use of overlords to that of setting up departments with terms of reference defining the division of responsibilities between the overall department and the sub-departments it is established to incorporate; e.g. the Department of the Environment combines under its general authority two hitherto separate departments with often overlapping functions and consequent problems of co-ordination and demarcation. The overall department becomes responsible for the achievement of the general policy objectives for which they share responsibility. In fact Tory policy in the early 1970s was aimed at integration as a means of co-ordination rather than the mere establishment of formal independent co-ordinating machinery.

26. Cabinet secretariat. The secretariat performs co-ordinating functions in addition to its Cabinet and Cabinet committee servicing functions. It achieves this principally through its duties of following up Cabinet decisions and making such decisions known to departmental ministers involved.

PROGRESS TEST 4

1. How may departments be classified? **(3)**
2. Explain the theory of allocation of functions. **(4–5)**
3. What are the main features of the White Paper on the Re-organisation of Government 1970? **(7–10)**
4. How are departments organised internally? **(14)**
5. What are the main problems of co-ordination of central government? **(15–16)**
6. Explain the role of the Cabinet as a co-ordinator. **(21–23)**

CHAPTER V

Central Administration
II: The Policy-Making Process

INTRODUCTION

1. Policy and administration. Public administration theorists were for a long period concerned with attempts conceptually to distinguish policy and administration. The distinction, which was probably based on a confusion of politics and administration, and the desire to keep the former out of the latter, has always been somewhat fictional. Nevertheless the theory of separation of these functions has been reflected considerably in British constitutional practice, particularly in the doctrine of ministerial responsibility, i.e. the minister is conceived of as being solely responsible on the political plane for policy-making and is aided by a neutral, non-policy-making bureaucracy which solely administers the policy decisions of the minister, and is effectively divorced from the intricacies of policy-making by its non-professional status.

NOTE: This distinction was not totally unrealistic in the period when legislatures still retained the initiative in policy-making and the executive branch of government was comparatively small and inexpert. However, the growth in administrative discretion, and the inability of legislatures to solve all problems by legislative means, has markedly shifted this emphasis. "The exercise of discretionary power, the making of value choices, is a characteristic and increasing function of administrators and bureaucrats; they are thus importantly engaged in politics." (W. S. Sayre, R. Carson and T. Harris, *Public Administration in Modern Society*, McGraw-Hill, 1963.)

2. The new emphasis. "The increasing volume and complexity of government has had two important results from the standpoint of administrative responsibility. It has shifted the initiative in legislation to the administration, and it has vastly increased the amount of legislating by the administration itself" (Simon). As will be seen (*see* **9–11**), this change in initiative gives the administration considerable power in choosing the goals and values by which its decisions will be guided.

POLICY-MAKING

3. The nature of policy. Policy has been defined as "a matter of either the desire for change or the desire to protect something from change" (Professor J. D B. Miller, *The Nature of Politics*, Penguin, 1965) or, more fully, as "policy-making occurs in the determination of major objectives, in the selection of methods of achieving these, and in the continuous adaptation of existing policies to the problems that face a government" (N. Johnson, "Who are the Policy Makers?" *Public Administration*, 1965).

There are therefore two principal features of policy, which may be identified as follows.

(*a*) Policy is concerned with either change (its dynamic aspect), or with the preservation of the *status quo* (its static aspect).

(*b*) There is no clear distinction between policy and administration and both contain dynamic elements. The existence of a passive executory administration is no longer a justifiable assumption.

4. Policy-making in a democracy. In a democracy, policy-making involves argument and criticism. It is thus possible to identify the following contributions to policy-making both internal and external to the governmental machine.

(*a*) *Party considerations*. The contribution of both government and opposition parties.

(*b*) *Government*. The hierarchical relationship of Cabinet, ministers and civil service.

(*c*) *External*. The effect of pressure groups, public opinion, party conferences, etc. (*see* XV).

5. The policy-making hierarchy. Four levels of policy-making hierarchy have been identified.

(*a*) *Political or general policy-making level*. This consists of the determination of major policy objectives in broad terms, these being manifested in the party political programmes. The effect of such broad policy is to provide a general framework within which effective policy may be worked out.

NOTE: It must be doubted whether such a broad policy classification can be truly regarded as policy at all, but consists rather of a comparatively undefined, non-binding set of ideals.

(b) *Executive policy*. This is regarded as the effective reduction of general or political policy into concrete, practical objectives, and manifests itself as Cabinet policy.

(c) *Administrative policy*. The form in which the ministerial administrator carries the executive policy into operation.

(d) *Technical policy*. The day-to-day policy adopted by officials in working out administrative policy.

6. Defects in the hierarchical theory. The following points should be noted.

(a) The theory tends to ignore inter-relations of various groups in the policy-making process, e.g. ministers and civil servants acting together.

(b) It fails to incorporate an effective definition of policy.

(c) It does not attempt to locate the point of effective policy-making i.e. to assess the relative importance of the various hierarchies.

(d) It fails completely to illustrate the upward movement in policy-making and regards policy-making as a downward progression from the general to the particular.

7. The elements of policy. Policy-making is effectively a two-part process.

(a) *Analysis and choice presentation*. This involves the primary determination of problem areas, definition of the issues involved therein and an examination of the methods of problem solving.

(b) *Decisions on policy*. This involves the making of the actual decision as to the implementation and choice of alternatives presented.

8. British constitutional theory. In theory the application of the elements of policy-making (*see* 7) implies a separation of people and of positions in time. It is, however, in the assessment of the relative importances of these functions that the location of policy-making power can be found. In strict theory the civil service has no policy-making power, but exists merely to advise ministers and to carry out policy determined by the minister.

LOCATION OF POWER

9. Power in the formulation role. The strategic position of the official and the comparative weakness of the minister have been summed up by Lord Bridges: "There is an early stage in any project when things are fluid; when, if you are in touch with those concerned and can get hold of the facts, it is fairly easy to influence decisions. But after a scheme has been worked on . . . it is very difficult to do anything but approve, or throw it overboard" (quoted by N. Johnson, "Who are the Policy Makers?" *Public Administration*, 1965, p. 284).

Thus the process of analysis and presentation may be divided into the following stages.

(*a*) The fluid stage where options are open and influence is of greatest importance.

(*b*) The post-research stage where alternatives are presented and modification and influence replaced by acceptance or rejection.

NOTE: It is thus in the preparation and presentation of alternatives (i.e. the true role of the civil servant) that the official may achieve something approaching absolute policy-making power. The role of a minister may thus be confined to exercising choices between presented alternatives.

10. The position of the minister. The weak position of the minister in policy-making is illustrated in the following ways.

(*a*) *Weakness of the constitutional doctrine*. The theory (*see* **8**) is based on the false assumption that a minister has time, energy and experience to master the great range of policy issues facing a modern department and can thus effectively control all aspects of that department's work.

(*b*) *Pressures on the minister*. The weakness of the minister might to an extent be alleviated if he was not overburdened with matters other than policy-making. However, he is concerned also with non-departmental matters, party political duties, official engagements, etc. These result in his having to rely heavily on advice from senior civil servants, and particularly from his Permanent Secretary (but note role of Senior Policy Advisers recommended by Fulton Committee—*see* VI. Such advice tends often to reach him in the form of a *fait accompli*.

(*c*) *Rejection of advice*. The minister's role is largely confined to choosing between alternatives presented to him, unless he is exceptionally astute or has outside advisers. Unless this is the case he is not likely to be aware of alternatives which have been rejected during the policy analysis stage. Thus it is probable that a minister is only presented with a real choice in the event of civil service disagreement.

11. Strategic position of civil servants. The following points should be noted.

(*a*) A minister will be unlikely to reject advice owing to his dependence on civil service co-operation, for the following reasons in particular:

(*i*) the officials may be his only source of advice (compare a French minister's personal "Cabinet");

(*ii*) officials are in the best position to carry out inter-departmental negotiations and liaison with the Treasury which may be necessary for the effective implementation of policy.

(*b*) Policy is often formed at inter-departmental meetings of civil servants, and minutes of ministerial proceedings are prepared by civil servants; the Private Secretary post is regarded as a promotion position and thus encouragement of frank relay back to the minister is discouraged; and the Permanent Secretary may tend to develop what he conceives to be the true role of his department, and is thus likely, consciously or unconsciously, to lead the minister.

"I have known a few cases where fairly senior officials have kept a Minister in the dark about the fact that there was quite a lot of debate further down the line" (Boyle).

(*d*) The official is in a strategic position (*see* **10**).

(*e*) The tradition of civil service anonymity protects the official from outside examination.

12. The role of the minister. Despite the predominance of the official the minister still retains an important role and, despite the pessimistic view expressed by R. H. S. Crossman ("In order to keep the monarchy constitutionally responsible for nothing we arranged that it could do no wrong—and likely made it impotent to do anything at all. Under our present system in Whitehall there is a danger of ministers going the same way"), the minister still retains importance in the following ways.

(a) A strong minister may be able to impose his will on his department.

(b) Ministers are still the "accountable persons" and the civil servants must therefore be constantly aware of the political environment in which they function.

(c) The legislative context of the ministerial role must be taken into account. Policy must manifest itself in legislation and a department thus must rely on the political ability of its minister to steer such legislation through the House.

(d) The role of the minister is strengthened by collective involvement in Cabinet, Cabinet committees, and *ad hoc* meetings with the Prime Minister.

Thus it is fallacious to regard a minister as playing a purely passive role in the policy-making process and his position must be viewed in the light of his political role and the exigencies thereof.

13. Strengthening the ministerial role. The minister's position *vis-à-vis* officials could be strengthened, however, by use of all or some of the following:

(a) provision of the minister with more expertise outside the single chain of command, e.g. greater use of "personal" appointments, use of a French style "Cabinet", etc.;

(b) an extension of the committee procedure of the House of Commons along the lines of the U.S. Congressional Committee of Inquiry system;

(c) direct access of the professional hierarchy in a department to the minister (*see* VI).

14. The role of the Treasury. Within the power structure of policy-making the Treasury is predominant on the official side. This domination is a result of the following:

(a) the representation on all inter-departmental committees of Treasury representatives;

(b) the role of the Treasury in the control of expenditure and the important relationship of policy and finance;

(c) the responsibility of the Treasury for fiscal and monetary policy which are the two main instruments of government economic policy.

15. Criticisms of civil servants as policy-makers. The following points should be noted:

(*a*) their tendency to compromise;
(*b*) their lack of professionalism;
(*c*) their lack of long-term strategies;
(*d*) their failure to make effective use of professionals.

(*See* also VI where these matters are more fully developed.)

16. Central Policy Review Staff. The White Paper on Reorganisation of Government, 1970, considered that the existing process of policy-making through inter-departmental committees needed to be reinforced by the development of a central strategy providing a framework within which the government's policies as a whole may be more effectively formulated.

The Central Policy Review Staff was in consequence established as an integral part of the Cabinet Office at the disposal of the government as a whole. Its task is to enable ministers to take better policy decisions by enabling them to work out the implications of their basic strategy in terms of policies in specific areas; to establish the relative priorities to be given to different sectors of their programmes; to identify those areas of policy in which new choices can be exercised; and to ensure that the implications of various courses are fully understood and analysed.

NOTE: This development, whilst improving the overall quality of decision-making, does not greatly affect the balance of power between ministers and civil servants, except to the extent that it makes ministers better informed. Colloquially known as the "think tank", it is a multi-disciplinary research team, and reflects the government's aim of developing an integrated policy framework. Its approach to research topics has been a selective one, and it has dealt with such wide ranging topics as government research and development, regional policy, the computer industry, Concorde, industrial growth. Its ongoing tasks, and this is probably its key policy function, are of a long-term strategic nature and include the social needs of the community over the next decade, the effects of taxation on business investment, and the significance of foreign control over industry.

A COMPARISON WITH LOCAL GOVERNMENT
POLICY-MAKING

17. Difficulty of precision. At least from an internal point of view central policy-making is comparatively clear cut compared with the practice in local government. The difficulty in arriving at a clear picture arises for the following reasons.

(a) Differences in size of local government units involve consequent differing relations between elected representatives and officials.

(b) More important figures are involved in the local government situation compared with the central position which is essentially a relationship between minister and Permanent Secretary.

(c) All members in local government have access to chief officers, whereas in central government the Opposition are denied access to senior civil servants.

(d) Personalities play a much greater role in local government.

18. Constitutional theory. This is the same as for the central government, i.e. officers advise and councillors decide policy. But this again ignores the following facts.

(a) Officers prepare matters for the council.

(b) Officers are the trained and experienced parties.

(c) Officers are in the best position to measure the impact of existing policy, to possess knowledge as to the adequacy of resources and to estimate the future effects of policy decisions.

19. Committee on Management in Local Government. Research carried out for the Committee identified various elements concerned in the initiation of policy, namely, "policy committees", party groups and intra-party influence group, individual committees, individual committee members, relationships between committee chairmen and chief officers, and the contributions of officers.

The Committee's report seemed unable to identify any readily definable source of policy initiation. In general its research showed a predominance of officer-initiated policy, this being explained as inevitable consequence of the technicalisation of local government work.

A comparison was drawn between "sowing seeds" and actually

defining policy, the responsibilities being those of officers and members respectively. However, a bald statement such as this could theoretically be applied also the central government situation and would tend to obliterate the realities of the situation.

20. The Bains Report. (*See* also XVII, **19–25**.) The Bains Working Group on Local Authority Management Structure reported in 1972, and most of the local authorities established on reorganisation in 1974 have accepted its proposals to a substantial extent. In essence its recommendations were based on the desirability of developing a Corporate Management approach in local government. In broad terms its main proposals may be summarised as follows.

(*a*) *Member structure.* On the member side it recommended a rationalisation of the committee structure, away from the concept of service committees and into programme committees dealing with related functions of the authority. At the apex of the committee structure there is now universally a policy and resources committee which sets the main strategic pattern for the local authority, though final policy decisions rest with the council. The policy and resources committee is supported by four sub-committees, namely land, personnel, finance, and performance review.

(*b*) *Officer structure.* The Bains Report did not advocate extensive reorganisation of the departmental structure, and indeed local authorities have proved resistant to suggestions of this nature. However the Report suggested, and this has generally been adopted, that co-ordination of policy on the officer side should be achieved through a system to some extent mirroring the member structure, viz. an officer's management team presided over by a non-departmental executive officer.

PROGRESS TEST 5

1. Compare the meanings of policy and administration. **(1, 2)**
2. What do you understand by policy-making? **(3, 4, 7)**
3. Comment on the hierarchical theory of policy-making. **(5, 6)**
4. Comment on the respective positions of the minister and civil servants in policy-making. **(9–13)**

5. What are the functions of the Central Policy Review Staff. **(16)**

6. Outline the policy-making process in local government. **(17–19)**

7. What were the main organisational recommendations of the Bains Report? **(20)**

CHAPTER VI

The Civil Service

INTRODUCTION

1. Definition. (The civil service was defined by the Tomlin Commission as "those servants of the Crown, other than political or judicial office holders, who are employed in a civil capacity, and whose remuneration is paid out of money provided by Parliament".)

2. Some underlying concepts. Any appraisal of the problems confronting the civil service must bear in mind the following points.

(*a*) Despite criticisms of organisation, selection and power, the civil service has an unparalleled achievement of impartiality, integrity and incorruptibility.

(*b*) The civil service is not on a parallel with organisations in the private sector and the tradition of political accountability and responsibility of political heads of departments necessarily results in a greater degree of bureaucratic procedure than might otherwise prevail. This manifests itself in a reluctance to delegate and consequent centralisation of decision-taking functions, in excessive and repeated checking of procedures and actions at lower levels and in a tendency to elevate the importance of maintaining the status quo.

(*c*) The real seat of effective policy-making power lies with the civil service (*see* V) and any discussion of the defects in the service must not be allowed to hide behind the practices of anonymity and ministerial responsibility.

(*d*) In the existing context of public administration the civil service must be judged as a management organisation and its effectiveness assessed as far as possible on principles which would be applied to management organisations, subject, however, to allowance for the constraints to which public administration is subject (*see* III).

3. The tasks of the civil service. The Fulton Committee stated the requirements of civil servants under modern conditions to be:

(a) practical judgment and negotiating skill;
(b) knowledge of economic and industrial factors;
(c) numerate skill;
(d) professionalism.

NOTE: The Committee distinguished as follows between the two types of "professionalism" in the context of the civil service. (1) Specialism in the professional capacity sense. The Committee considered that the civil service had been consistently neglectful of this, and in particular had failed to give specialists the equivalent status and responsibilities they would have enjoyed in private business, particularly by the policy of organising specialists in separate hierarchies and by reserving policy and financial control to generalist administrators. It will be seen that the English Committee (*see* **27–28**) took the attitude that in 1977 this problem had not been adequately overcome. (2) Professionalism among generalists in the sense that generalist administrators tended to lack expertise in any particular area, and that this consequently inhibited effective policy-making, prevented fundamental policy evaluation, and led to inadequate relationships with outside organisations.

HISTORICAL DEVELOPMENT

4. The Northcote-Trevelyan Report 1854. The *Report on Organisation of the Permanent Civil Service* was of great importance in establishing the underlying principles of the civil service until the post-Fulton Committee reforms in the late 1960s to early 1970s. Until this latter period the civil service was largely anchored by the Northcote-Trevelyan concepts of career service and predominance of the generalist, despite the fact that fundamental changes had taken place in the nature of government since 1854, and in particular:

(a) the change from passive regulation to active participation;
(b) the development of new decision-making techniques;
(c) rapid technological progress;
(d) the blurring of public and private sector functions;

(*e*) the extension of the decision-making time factor through complexity, etc.;

(*f*) increasing international involvement.

5. Defects prior to Fulton. The Fulton Committee was appointed in 1966 to "examine the structure, recruitment and management, including training, of the Home Civil Service, and to make recommendations". Stated briefly the major deficiencies found by the Committee were:

(*a*) the overriding predominance of the generalist philosophy;

(*b*) the work impeding factors of the class system;

(*c*) lack of opportunities, responsibilities and authority given to specialist groupings;

(*d*) inadequacy of the use of skilled managers;

(*e*) inadequacy of contact between the service and the public;

(*f*) inadequate personnel management.

6. The Fulton Committee recommendations. These may be examined in outline under the classifications of:

(*a*) recruitment and training;

(*b*) mobility and career service;

(*c*) the structure of departments;

(*d*) the structure of the overall service;

(*e*) the central management of the civil service;

(*f*) the civil service and the community.

7. Recruitment and training. The principal recommendations of the Committee were:

(*a*) the integration of responsibilities for recruitment and training;

(*b*) the establishment of a new Civil Service Department;

(*c*) recruitment should be for a specific function;

(*d*) more emphasis on recruitment by departments involved;

(*e*) the establishment of a civil service college.

8. Mobility and career service. The Committee were anxious to preserve the career service nature of the civil service and they felt it led to a professional and experienced service; it encouraged loyalty; and it led to less constraints on giving forthright and impartial opinions. The Committee however recommended that:

(*a*) advantages would accrue from temporary and short-term

appointments and from an interchange of staff with industry and commerce;

(b) there should be greater consideration given to facilitating movements into and out of the service.

9. Departmental structure.

The Committee considered that the common organisational need of defining responsibility and decision-making authority in the civil service was difficult as decisions invariably had to be referred for confirmation to an unnecessarily high level, and that delegation was difficult due to decisions often overlapping departments. Nonetheless they recommended that:

(a) accountable management should be established in order to identify parts of an organisation to which cost and other performance measurement might be applied;

(b) high level management services and techniques should be applied;

(c) long-term planning and research units should be established and these should be responsible for the identification and study of long-term problems; suggesting appropriate policies; and referencing short-term decisions to future developments.

10. Civil service structure.

The committee considered that the defects in the then existing structure were that the class system was invalid; the occupational divisions between separate divisions and specialisms caused strain; the structure prevented the most efficient use of staff; the structure led to the inefficient organisation of work; effective job analysis was inhibited; and accountable management was made difficult. In response to these criticisms the Committee made two fundamental proposals for change.

(a) Class divisions should be abolished and a continuous grading structure substituted for each occupational group.

(b) The best man for the job must apply to the civil service irrespective of occupational groupings or educational qualifications.

NOTE: These recommendations implied the need for a unified classless structure. A number of successive grading levels embracing all jobs in the service was required, and the salary range in each grade should be relatively broad and overlapping between grades.

11. Central management of the civil service. Prior to Fulton the Treasury was responsible for the central management of the service. This function was discharged through the Pay and Management Group. This, however, was never a fully developed body with overall management responsibility, e.g. recruitment was shared with the Civil Service Commission, and responsibility for personnel management and management services tended to be more advisory than directive.

Consequently the Fulton Committee recommended that two major institutional changes were required.

(*a*) Responsibility for recruitment, selection and other functions of central management should be brought together in a single department.

(*b*) The expanded and unified management functions should be made the responsibility of a new department created specifically for that purpose, particularly as central management is not an appropriate function for a central finance department such as the Treasury.

12. The civil service and the community. The Committee advocated greater participation in the decision-making process; that civil service anonymity was no longer a valid principle; and on a broader scale that Ministers should become more involved in the decision-making process, e.g. by the use of personal appointments and senior policy advisers.

THE PRESENT STRUCTURE

13. The Civil Service Department. Among the first steps taken to implement the Fulton Committee Report was the establishment of a Civil Service Department to take over the Treasury's responsibilities. Although theoretically under the direct control of the Prime Minister, day-to-day responsibility is in the hands of another cabinet minister, often the Leader of the House of Lords. The Department's own staff is headed by a permanent secretary with the title of Head of the Home Civil Service. Although not part of the Department the Civil Service Commission retains its title and some degree of independence in the administration of recruitment.

The main functions of the department are as follows.

(a) *Personnel management functions.* The Department lays down the policy on recruitment, training, promotion, staff welfare, and retirement. The general allocation of manpower, pay, pensions, and conditions of service also come within its scope.

(b) *Methods of management.* The Department has general responsibility for developing new managerial techniques within the civil service, and to this end it provides a management consultancy service. It also covers computers, data processing and other technical developments.

14. Staffing structure. At the beginning of 1971 the executive and clerical classes were merged into a new administration group, which also took in all administrative grades up to and including assistant secretaries. The grading throughout the group now provides a continuous "ladder" from top to bottom, without the class barriers that hitherto existed. There remain however different points of entry into the system, being geared to levels of educational attainment.

15. Under secretaries and above. The administration group consists of some 230,000 employees, of which one-quarter would be equivalent to the old executive class. The remaining 750 posts are occupied by members of the old administrative class and have been absorbed into a single rationalised pay and grading structure.

16. Departmental classes. These consist of certain officers carrying out functions, although of a similar level to that performed by the administration group, are of a comparatively specialist nature, e.g. customs officials and tax inspectors.

17. Scientific and specialist groups. These groups consist of civil servants with technical and professional qualifications and functions, e.g. scientists, engineers, architects and statisticians. In 1978 the classes were in the process of rationalisation and amalgamation.

18. Allocation of functions. Although the civil service is now "classless" an examination of the functions of the old classes gives some indication of the type of work carried out at particular levels in the civil service.

(a) The *administrative* class which now corresponds broadly with the top of the administration group, and with undersecretaries and above, though predominantly with the latter, was concerned broadly with the exercise of financial control over departmental work, the development, setting out and execution of government policy, and with what might generally be described as "management functions".

(b) The old *executive* class was principally responsible for the more important work of supply and accounting departments, for casework, and for matters of internal organisation and control. In addition executive officers were concerned with the supervision and management of large blocks of clerical work, the management of local and regional offices, and such important matters as government accounting, contract negotiation, organisation and method work, and automatic data processing.

(c) The *clerical* class was concerned essentially with the performance of routine day-to-day functions.

19. Training. The Management Personnel Training Division of the Civil Service Department examines and reassesses the training needs of the civil service. It meets itself those needs which can be catered for centrally, otherwise it gives advice to training officers and instructors who are attached to each Ministry and Department. Training needs are satisfied either by residential courses at the Civil Service College, established in 1970, or through internal departmental training.

PARTICULAR PROBLEM AREAS

20. Weakness of line management functions. The "line manager" in the civil service is subject to the following constraints which would be very rare in a commercial or industrial undertaking.

(a) *Motivational constraints.* Unlike the line manager in a non-public administration context, the line manager in the civil service is deprived of many of the motivational incentives and sanctions normally associated with his post, e.g. he does not have powers to hire and fire, to award bonuses, to promote, etc. The only "establishment" type function he can exercise is in respect of the annual employee report which again is modified in effect as a result of the civil service convention of "fair play".

(b) *Financial control weaknesses.* Where financial authority is delegated to persons in line management situations such persons are subject to constraints imposed by central management functions. This results in excessive caution, reference of decisions to the highest level to guarantee support for decisions and excessive detailing of decisions.

(c) *Management control and techniques*. The concept of management control in the civil service is given limited interpretation. Unlike an industrial manager, who may be responsible for the organisation and cost effectiveness therein, the civil service manager exercises a passive role in controlling costs based on a public accountability for expenditure basis, rather than a positive approach of using management techniques to improve departmental efficiency. There is comparatively little encouragement in the system to express quantitatively required standards of achievement.

21. The specialist-versus-generalist controversy. Although the controversy is somewhat mitigated in respect of the civil service as a result of the Fulton Report it still merits serious consideration in that:

(a) the English Committee Report (*see* **27–28**) suggests that the higher posts in the civil service are still filled by generalist administrators, and there is still a bias in recruitment in this direction;

(b) the controversy goes beyond the civil service and may be seen as having broad application in public administration, particularly in the local government service.

22. The theory. The theory of the preference for the generalist administrator is that their broad academic background effectively enables them to reflect the views of their political head, who in turn is non-specialist, and that, by virtue of their in-service training, they are able to deal with a wide range of matters.

23. The case for the administrator. The following points should be noted.

(a) The "administrative function" it is claimed does not depend on the possession of particularised technical expertise. "Since administrative decisions are never of the same character as technical decisions, the technical expert does not in principle have any merits over other persons as a performer of the administrative function" (Paul Meyer, *Administrative Organisation*).

(b) The specialist is likely to give undue weight to technical considerations.

(*c*) Specialists have a greater tendency to ride "hobby horses".

(*d*) The view was expressed in the Northcote-Trevelyan Report, that men who have followed no formal technical education or who have exercised no specific business background "will generally be found in business of every profession superior . . . to those devoted to the special studies of their calling".

24. The case for the specialist. The following points should be noted.

(*a*) The concept of the "administrative" function (*see* **25**) tends to underestimate the considerable technical element that may be contained in what is superficially considered to be a purely administrative decision.

(*b*) Technical knowledge may often prove more important than mere administrative skill alone.

(*c*) There is no reason, as illustrated by the experience of the French Civil Service (*see* **29–33** below) to assume that a specialist is incapable of acquiring administrative techniques.

(*d*) There has been a failure of generalists to identify the key long-term problems of administration.

(*e*) Administrative skill nowadays is in fact a specialist matter involving the application of sophisticated management techniques, and thus, of itself, requiring specialised training and experience.

25. Is there an "administrative function"? As has been seen a key element in the generalist case has been the ability to identify a separate administrative function. Essentially the case for reserving the higher policy-making and control positions for generalist administrators rests upon the presupposition of the existence of this separate function. This has been defined as the "bringing together of the disparate issues involved in taking major decisions of policy, advising on what the decisions should be, and subsequently putting them into effect" (evidence of First Division Association to the Fulton Committee). British practice has consequently been to evolve a false distinction between administration and management to the detriment of the management role. This view of administration as an art rather than a science leads to the relative disrespect for management control and operational techniques.

26. The civil service and economic policy-making. Economic policy-making at the official level is the result of the combined effort of various officials, namely, administrators, economic advisers, and administrators who are at the same time economists. In practice, however, because of numerical and hierarchical factors, there has tended to be a concentration of authority in this field in the hands of the generalist administrators compared with the authority wielded by the "irregulars", i.e. the professional economists. Despite the drafting into the civil service of large numbers of economists, particularly during the Labour administration of 1964–70, mistakes were made which prevented the redress of the balance in favour of the professionals, and this position still applies to a considerable extent despite the recommendations of the Fulton Committee.

(a) The specialist economists were spread too thinly between departments, and generally too low in the administrative hierarchy to give them either collective or individual authority.

(b) The tendency still remains to leave generalist administrators in the final decision-making position in the hierarchy.

(c) Considerable importance was still attached to the non-economist lobbies.

THE ENGLISH COMMITTEE REPORT

27. The English Committee. The English Committee, technically part of the House of Commons Expenditure Committee, mounted in 1977 the first proper and independent inquiry into how the civil service had implemented the reforms thought essential by the Fulton Committee. Its report (the Eleventh Report of the Expenditure Committee) was highly critical and in general terms it considered that the Civil Service had failed to implement the major recommended reforms (*see* also **34–37** below). The report was significant in that it represented the first investigation into the public service by a parliamentary, as distinct from governmental, committee for 104 years.

28. The main recommendations.

(a) Responsibility for efficiency and manpower requirements of the service should be returned from the Civil Service Department to the Treasury. The basic reason for this view was that, in the Committee's opinion, there had occurred an indefensible separation of control over public service expenditure, exercised by the Treasury, from responsibility for efficiency and manpower requirements, exercised by the Civil Service Department.

(b) Parliamentary committees should be established specifically related to departments and manned by back-benchers.

(c) The doctrine of ministerial responsibility should be relaxed with reference to accountable units so that civil servants could be publicly accountable for management, but not political, decisions.

(d) The present limit on ministerial advisers of two per Cabinet member should be scrapped and the ministers should be free to adopt any organisation they think fit.

A COMPARISON WITH THE FRENCH CIVIL SERVICE

29. A background. In considering the significance of differences in organisation and operation between the two civil services the following background points must be borne in mind.

(a) The two civil services had developed against different concepts of the role of the state; namely, the British civil service developed during the period of *laissez-faire* and the "nightwatchman" theory of the role of the state, whereas the French civil service developed in a state where there has been for a considerable period marked emphasis on state intervention on a wide scale.

(b) The French system of government involves considerable administrative de-concentration, including the running of what in Britain would be considered local government services and consequently involves considerable functional specialisation and expertise.

(c) French higher education is more career-orientated than the British system. The use of civil service schools and specialised post-entry training in schools attached to ministries results in the training of the French specialist classes taking place outside the traditional university system.

(d) France has never experienced or encouraged the separation between careers in public administration, business management and technology which is found in Britain.

(e) The policy of the French technical schools is from the outset to recognise the need for the training of specialists to encompass both technical and administrative training.

30. The use of specialists. The French civil service places predominant reliance on prescribed qualifications. These qualifications in specialists take the form, however, of civil service rather than professional body qualifications as in the British specialist classes. In addition, in France most *corps* (*see* **31**(*b*)) are truly departmental and specialise and carry responsibility for specific areas of departmental work. However, French specialists are regarded as both technical personnel and potential administrators and both technical and administrative corps members may be promoted to administrative positions.

31. Structure of the service. The French civil service is structured in the following ways.

(*a*) *Classes*. The service is horizontally divided into four classes, based essentially on educational background, which deal with broad functions, e.g. Category A deals with "policy and direction". Promotion barriers exist both between and within classes, e.g. between the divisions of Category A into higher and secondary corps.

(*b*) *Corps*. All civil servants are appointed to corps within which their particular careers lie. In comparison, classes have relatively little importance. Corps have been defined as groups of civil servants governed by the same regulations and qualifications for the same grades. Each corps is a watertight unit.

(*c*) *Services*. These represent the vertical divisions of the civil service. A service consists of a series of vertically related corps, and results in the unification of policy-making and field services through the top management sections in Paris.

(*d*) *Grades*. These exist within each corps.

32. Recruitment and promotion. Recruitment is generally based on examinations and little emphasis is placed on character, proven ability, etc. In the technical corps, examinations are usually theoretical in order to test intellectual ability. Recruitment to the corps in Class A requires admission to post-entry schools, i.e. the National School of Administration or the École Polytechnique, and graduation from these.

Promotion is by "objective" examination procedures to the higher corps. Within corps, promotion is usually by seniority, though at the higher grade level procedures are more formalised.

33. Conclusion. The following characteristics of the French civil service may be identified:

(*a*) career orientation;
(*b*) allegiance to corps rather than to the service;
(*c*) use of specialists as administrators (*see* **30** above);
(*d*) little distinction between technical and advisory functions;
(*e*) movement in and out of the service is common, particularly in the higher corps.

IMPLEMENTATION OF THE FULTON PROPOSALS

34. Government White Paper. The English Committee was very critical of the extent to which the Fulton proposals had been implemented (*see* **27–28** above). The Government published a White Paper on Civil Service Reform (1978) which appeared to be less pessimistic than the English Committee, but which blatantly fails to answer the major criticisms of that committee. The Fulton Committee reforms essentially centred on the concept of professionalism, the need to overhaul recruitment, and the need to create greater opportunities for non-graduates and specialists.

The White Paper stated that "the acceptance of Fulton resulted in a number of radical changes in the organisation and management of the civil service". On the other hand Lord Crowther Hunt commented "in general, the civil service has implemented those parts of Fulton it liked and which added to its power, and failed to implement the ideas that would have made it more professional, and more accountable to Parliament and the public". It is thus necessary to attempt an assessment of these conflicting views.

35. Quantifiable results.

(*a*) *Civil service should be less "Oxbridge" dominated.* In fact the "Oxbridge" graduates as a proportion of external recruits to the administrative grade increased from 62 per cent (1966–8) to 63 per cent (1975–7).

> NOTE: It is also clear that where recruitment is from other universities it fails to reflect the composition of such universities, being heavily weighted in favour of those with a public school background.

(*b*) *Civil service intake to be less dominated by arts graduates.*

Arts graduates as a proportion of recruits to the administrative grades only decreased from 59 per cent (1966–8) to 56 per cent (1975–7).

(c) *More specialists should get top jobs.* The background of undersecretaries and above was in the proportion 62:38 per cent, generalists to specialists, in 1970, and in 1978 had only changed to 59:41 per cent.

(d) *More qualified accountants in the civil service.* The number of qualified accountants had only increased from 309 in 1967 to 367 in 1978.

(e) *Substantial exchange of staff with industry and local government.* The number of civil servants seconded to industry, commerce and local government had increased from twelve in 1968 to twenty-five in 1975.

36. Comments on the statistics.

(a) The apparent biases in recruitment of elite administrators were still as evident as ever.

(b) The hold of generalists on the eight hundred most senior jobs at under-secretary level and above was still maintained.

(c) The number of accountants, although growing in absolute numbers, was growing less slowly than the civil service as a whole.

(d) The flow of civil servants to commerce and industry on secondment was misleading. The White Paper pointed out that "the rise in these figures . . . indicates an improvement in data flow from the departments rather than a real increase in activity". Even allowing for this the figures involved were extremely low in relation to the total number of civil servants employed.

37. The English Committee. The committee stressed in particular the need for:

(a) more professionalism;
(b) a complete overhaul of administrative training;
(c) greater control over Whitehall by ministers and by Parliament.

38. Defects in the White Paper. The crucial criticism of the White Paper was that it totally failed to respond to many of the major issues raised by the English Committee, in particular, the following.

(a) *Recruitment.* No response appeared to the English Committee's comment that "it looks as if the Civil Service Commission not only reinforces an Oxford and Cambridge bias, but (even where it does take from other universities, tends to prefer public school boys and so) also creates a bias which either does not exist in other universities or is much smaller there".

(b) *A classless civil service.* The Wilson Government accepted the Fulton recommendation that all barriers to career progress in the civil service should be scrapped and a "unified grading structure" created. However unified grading had only so far been applied to the eight hundred senior civil service posts. The Committee commented that "for reasons that are not very clear, progress on this ceased in October 1975. Incomes policy was given as one reason but does not seem to be wholly relevant and another reason given that it would take the time of staff inspectors, seems merely to mean that this matter is given no priority".

(c) *Professional accountants.* "The Fulton recommendation on the employment of accountants on an increasing scale in the civil service does not seem to have had much effect".

(d) *Cash limits.* These "render the present division of responsibility between the Treasury and the Civil Service Department obsolete; by investing the Treasury with an interest in the efficiency of departments, they destroy the 'raison d'etre' for a second department which is also concerned with efficiency".

(e) *Ministerial power.* "Many departments are large and it is not difficult to push forward policies without a Minister's knowledge . . . further it is often said to be extremely difficult to launch a new policy initiative which is not to the liking of the Department . . . there seems to us to be no justification for any of these practices".

PROGRESS TEST 6.

1. What is meant by "professionalism" in the context of the civil service?   (3).

2. Outline the changes in government which affected the role of the civil service between 1854 and the Report of the Fulton Committee.   (4)

3. What did the Fulton Committee consider to be the main defects in the civil service?   (5).

4. Outline the main recommendations of the Fulton Committee.   (6–12).

5. What is the role of the Civil Service Department?   (13).

6. How has the staffing structure of the civil service altered since the Report of the Fulton Committee?   (14–17).

7. What are the main constraints imposed on a "line manager" in the civil service?   (20).

8. Compare the cases for the generalist administrator and the specialist in the civil service.   (21–25).

9. What were the main recommendations in the English Committee Report?   (27–28).

10. Compare the structure of the British civil service with that of the French civil service.   (29–33).

11. To what extent have the main recommendations of the Fulton Committee not been implemented?   (34–36).

12. Outline the defects in the 1978 White Paper on Civil Service Reform.   (38).

CHAPTER VII

Bureaucracy

CHARACTERISTICS OF BUREAUCRACY

1. A definition of bureaucracy. The difficulty in arriving at an adequate definition of bureaucracy is the necessary elimination of certain derogatory or subjective and emotive descriptions. Various meanings which have been given to the term include the following.

(*a*) *Institutional meaning.* The term "bureaucracy" may refer to government by officials as opposed to government by elected representatives. Alternatively, it may be used to indicate that, although representative government exists, the dominant role is held by the officials. These definitions, however, tend to be inadequate in that they fail to distinguish those common situations where government consists of a combination of elected and non-elected members and officials.

(*b*) *Activity of officials.* In contrast a definition may be attempted from the aspect of what officials do or how they behave. In this respect the following interpretations exist.

(*i*) *Derogatory.* The synonomous use of "bureaucracy" and "red tape", resulting from the real and supposed difficulties of dealing with the official environment.

(*ii*) *Regulated system.* A regulated administrative system operating through complex interrelated organs.

(*iii*) *Methodological.* A study of methods based on either (*i*) or (*ii*) above.

For the purpose of this chapter the definition at (*b*)(*ii*) above as a regulated system will be adopted. This is due to its objective and analytical nature, the other definitions being associated with subjective or disparaging overtones. Bureaucracy is thus conceived of as a form of organisation.

2. Weber's definition of bureaucracy. Max Weber, the German sociologist, principally developed the organisational definition of bureaucracy, and conceived of the concept in two aspects, namely:

(*a*) the social mechanism that maximises efficiency in administration;

(*b*) a form of social organisation with specific characteristics. Peter M. Blau has described this social organisation as "institutionalised strategies for the achievement of administrative objectives by the concerted efforts of many officials" (*Bureaucracy in Modern Society*, Random House).

3. Weber's characteristics of bureaucracy. Weber specified the following characteristics or conditions that an organisation must possess before properly being called a bureaucracy.

(*a*) The regular activities required for the purposes of the structure are distributed in fixed ways as official duties.

(*b*) Specified spheres of competence have been marked off as part of a systematic division of labour.

(*c*) The official is subject to strict and systematic discipline and control in the conduct of his office.

(*d*) All operations are governed by a consistent system of abstract rules.

(*e*) There is consistency in the application of the rules to specific cases.

(*f*) The organisation of offices follows the principles of hierarchy, i.e. each lower office is under the control and supervision of a higher one.

(*g*) Officials are subject to authority only with respect to their impersonal official obligations.

(*h*) Candidates are selected on the basis of technical qualifications. In the most rational cases this will be tested by examinations, or guaranteed by diplomas certifying technical competence, etc.

(*i*) Being a bureaucratic official constitutes a career, and there is a system of promotion according to seniority or merit, or both.

4. Weber's conclusions. Weber concluded that a fully developed bureaucracy has the advantages of speed, precision, unambiguity, continuity, discretion, unity, strict subordination, and reduction of friction and of material and personal costs. He considered that its specific nature develops more perfectly the more it is dehumanised, i.e. "the more completely it succeeds in eliminating from official business all purely personal, irrational, and emotional elements which escape calculation".

The organisation conceived by Weber is therefore designed to achieve a rational orientation towards tasks which are conducive to efficient administration.

5. Etzioni's view. Etzioni considered that organisations are characterised by the following:

(*a*) divisions of labour, of power, and of communication responsibilities, such divisions being deliberately planned to achieve certain goals;

(*b*) the presence of power centres which control the concentrated effort of the organisation and continuously review its performance and repattern its structure, where necessary, to increase its efficiency;

(*c*) the classification of personnel.

This view is based on Weber's classical view of bureaucracy.

BUREAUCRATIC PROCEDURE

6. Nature. Bureaucratic procedure dictates a course of action governed by a prescribed set of rules, in order to achieve uniformity. Such rules are abstract in order to guide the different courses of action necessary for the accomplishment of the organisation's objectives in diverse conditions. The rules become more detailed at the lower points in the organisation's hierarchy, though at the point of execution modification may be necessary in the interests of administrative efficiency.

7. Modification. This involves modifying procedures to focus them on their intended objectives and on existing conditions. Such modification may be induced by internal or external factors and may involve the following.

(*a*) *Redefinition*. The sacrifice of one objective of procedure in order to achieve another more effectively.

(*b*) *Amplification*. The redirection of operations towards objectives which are in danger of neglect.

NOTE: Modification gives bureaucracy a dynamic aspect and enables an organisation to serve the needs it was created to serve.

8. "Sine ira et studio." Weber stated that bureaucratic officials will approach the public "in a spirit of formalistic impersonality without hatred or passion, and hence without affection or enthusiasm". He conceived of this requirement as intended to assure equitable treatment of clients, and rational rather than emotionally dominated administration.

In practice, however, this approach is not always operable as demonstrated by Blau in his research on the treatment of Negro clients by U.S. agencies. However, personal motives and prejudices may largely be eliminated by an evaluation system of focusing interest, e.g. by statistical records.

THE CASE AGAINST BUREAUCRACY

9. Nature of the case. The principles of the case against bureaucracy stem from its supposed mechanistic nature, i.e. its regimentation and predictability. Thus, in essence, the very advantages claimed by Weber are turned against bureaucracy by its critics.

10. Disadvantages of bureaucracy. The following points should be noted.

(*a*) Men in bureaucracy fulfil merely segmental roles over which they have no control.

(*b*) In consequence, they have little or no opportunity to exercise individual judgment, with the result that an employee feels separated from his work.

(*c*) In order to be effective, bureaucratic personnel must behave consistently and follow regulations strictly. This automatically limits a bureaucrat's capacity to adapt to changing circumstances not envisaged by those who drew up the rules.

(*d*) The general rules which may make for overall efficiency produce inefficiency and injustice in individual cases.

(*e*) The impersonal treatment of clients envisaged by Weber has harmful effects *vis-à-vis* such clients.

(*f*) Weber's view that bureaucrats should not become closely involved in personal relations with colleagues has undesirable practical effects and according to research carried out by Blau (*The Dynamics of Bureaucracy*, Univ. of Chicago Press, 1955), the "ritualistic" behaviour of bureaucrats stems more from the instability of established social relationships within the organisation than from over-identification with rules.

(*g*) The key limit on the efficiency of bureaucratic administration lies in the difficulty of coping with uncertainty and change. Bureaucracy thus rests upon tasks being convertible into routine. Blau has pointed out, however, that unfavourable conditions of operation may in fact generate favourable attitudes to change.

"Nobody can at the same time be a correct bureaucrat and an innovator. Progress is precisely that which the rules and regulations did not foresee; it is necessarily outside the field of bureaucratic activities." (Von Mises.)

NOTE: Blau (*see* (*f*) above) considered that a categorical statement as to the antipathy between bureaucracy and innovation was not justified. He found that bureaucratic operations can be instrumental in promoting social change, but that a member of the bureaucracy is not capable of changing procedures on his individual initiative.

11. Chester I. Barnard's view. Chester Barnard criticised Weber for failing to analyse and compare the correspondence of behaviour in organisations with organisational blueprints. In particular he failed to account for the fact that in the course of operations new elements arise in the structure which will effectively influence subsequent operations. Such "informal organisations" were considered by Barnard to be necessary to the operation of formal organisations as means of communication, cohesion, etc.

12. The failure of bureaucracy. Warren G. Bennis (*The Functions of the Executive*, Harvard Univ. Press, 1938) considered that bureaucracy no longer works, and advanced the following reasons.

(*a*) It suffices only for simple tasks under simple conditions. In existing conditions of change Bennis considers that "survival is dependent on the institutionalisation of perpetual change . . . and democracy becomes necessary".

(*b*) Change is accelerated by the growth of science, research and development activities, and intellectual technology. In addition the increase in transactions with social institutions, e.g. trade unions, has a profound influence and militates against the conditions suitable for the effective working of bureaucracy (i.e. stable conditions of environment are displaced).

(*c*) Formal education of employees alienates them from bureaucracy. In particular, hierarchy and bureaucracy are anathema to the professional. In addition a scientific attitude can only flourish in a democratic environment.

NOTE: Bennis considered that future organisations will tend to consist of temporary project teams to solve specific problems, with executives functioning as co-ordinators rather than as hierarchical supervisors.

13. Personal factors. A further disadvantage of bureaucracy is that personal factors associated with it tend to reinforce reaction against change. In particular, the following should be noted.

(*a*) An organisation set up to achieve change may have its objectives compromised by administrators in the organisation if the achievement of such objectives tends to threaten their tenure or the overall stability of the organisation.

(*b*) Identification with existing bureaucratic apparatus creates a tendency to sanctify procedures, and thus to resist changes in them even though conditions may call for such adjustment.

BUREAUCRACY AND PUBLIC ADMINISTRATION

14. Public administration as a large-scale organisation. Initially, it is important not to confuse defects in bureaucracy with defects in large-scale organisation. Defects in co-ordination and organisation inherent in large-scale organisations may apply whether the organisation is bureaucratic or not. In addition, criticisms of complexity of organisation, the subordination of the individual, conformity, and the stifling of initiative must be accepted as applicable to most large-scale organisations and not merely as characteristic of bureaucracy.

15. Efficient public administration. The more disadvantageous effects of public administration may be diminished by the presence of certain features:

(*a*) effective external political control;
(*b*) flexibility of organisation;
(*c*) good leadership and management;
(*d*) maximum internal delegation;
(*e*) just personnel management;

(*f*) maximum internal co-operation;

(*g*) continuous review of, and research into, objectives, methods and results;

(*h*) a professional morale antipathetic to bureaucratic methods;

(*i*) effective publicity;

(*j*) widespread outside understanding.

16. The civil service and bureaucracy. The civil service has been accused of containing a "bureaucratic, hierarchically organised, and tightly knit élite" (A. M. Hanson and M. Walles, *Governing Britain*, Fontana, 1973). On the other hand, it has been stated that "bureaucracy is a means of institutionalising clear, universal and impartial procedures for the administration of authority . . . infinitely preferable to most of its historical alternatives". What must therefore be considered is the extent to which the British civil service combines the more preferable aspects of bureaucracy with subjugation of the more harmful aspects. In this respect two important aspects must be borne in mind as background, rendered all the more important in industrial society, namely:

(*a*) the administration of modern technology greatly magnifies the tasks of administrative bodies;

(*b*) the process of decision-making becomes increasingly technical as the amount of necessary information multiplies.

In order to determine the bureaucratic elements in the British civil service it is proposed to analyse its nature against Weber's principles, and then to consider it in the light of the principles of efficient public administration outlined above (*see* **17**).

17. Comparison with Weber's principles. Superficially, the British civil service accords with many of Weber's characteristics, yet close analysis reveals that in actual practice such accordance is not predominant. The following points should be noted.

(*a*) The civil service follows the principles of hierarchy with supervision and control of lower offices by higher ones. In practice this control tends to be less than real, with considerable independence of action delegated to individual civil servants, though often exclusively at higher levels.

(*b*) Selection of candidates on the ground of technical qualifications determined by examination, etc., has long been a cardinal principle of civil service entry, at least prior to interview stage. However, such entry has not been exclusively predetermined on the grounds of technical competence and qualifications.

(c) The systematic division of labour exists to a large extent and was typified in particular by the old class system and the strict division between specialist and generalist. However, within classes the regular rotation of staff (again largely administrative class) operated against this.

(d) The civil service constitutes a career for most officials, with little or no movement between the service and industry, as exists for example in the U.S.A. civil service.

(e) Detailing of duties in specific form certainly exists at most executive levels and is particularly prevalent amongst lower grades.

(f) As has been explained in V, the policy-making function of higher civil servants is a marked departure from bureaucratic practice. However, this is limited to a comparative view of the very top ranks.

(g) The emphasis on public accountability contributes to bureaucratic procedure by enforcing double checking, reference to higher authority, etc.

18. Comparison with principles of efficiency. The consistency of the civil service with these principles is largely dealt with elsewhere in the book, as follows:

(a) effective political control (see II);
(b) flexibility of organisation, etc. (see VI);
(c) effective publicity and outside understanding (see VI);
(d) leadership and management, etc. (see VI).

19. Conclusions. The bureaucratic tendencies in the British civil service are probably overestimated and exist more at lower grade levels, though of course this has effects resulting in public frustration.

A key to principles of efficient administration and reaction against bureaucratic tendencies lies in the adoption of the Fulton recommendations (see VI), which aim at increasing efficiency, enlarging external relations, minimising hierarchical tendencies, bettering personnel management, and generally increasing the flexibility and initiative of the service.

PROGRESS TEST 7

1. What is meant by "bureaucracy"? **(1, 2)**

2. What did Weber consider to be the characteristics and advantages of bureaucracy? **(3, 4)**

3. Outline the case against bureaucracy. **(9–13)**

4. How far do you consider the civil service to be a bureaucracy? **(16–18)**

CHAPTER VIII

Public Expenditure

INTRODUCTION

1. The various aspects of public expenditure. Public expenditure may be regarded from three main differing viewpoints.

(*a*) *Legal.* This involves ensuring that public expenditure is incurred only in respect of those matters for which there is express approval, and then only within specified limits.

(*b*) *Managerial.* This is the control aspect which consists of ensuring the efficient carrying out of policies and the elimination of the waste of public funds.

(*c*) *Strategic.* This means devoting resources to objectives that are most effective in reaching goals which have been predetermined after critical policy analysis.

2. Public expenditure and Parliament. The legal framework of parliamentary involvement consists of the following.

(*a*) Estimates of expenditure are presented to Parliament, and, where appropriate, supplementary estimates.

(*b*) Estimates are divided into "votes" in respect of particular items of expenditure, and all votes in particular fields are grouped together in "classes" of which there are twelve in all, e.g. defence estimates.

(*c*) Parliament theoretically scrutinises the votes, and at this point could exercise the managerial function. This, however, is in fact precluded by lack of time and the preference for treating Supply Days as occasions for debates on matters of general policy. In addition, votes are insufficiently detailed to allow effective exercise of this function.

(*d*) Votes, when approved, go into the Appropriation Act.

(*e*) The Appropriation Accounts are audited by the Exchequer and Audit department, and are reported to the House with the report of the Comptroller and Auditor General. These are then referred to the Public Accounts Committee (*see* **4** below).

(*f*) The report of the Public Accounts Committee completes the cycle.

NOTE: Although concern has been expressed at the perfunctory examination which the estimates receive it would appear that the procedure suits both government and opposition parties, as formal approval with minimum discussion permits concentration on political-capital-making aspects. In addition the House exercises more effective detailed control through the medium of its supporting committees.

CONTROL THROUGH COMMITTEE STRUCTURE

3. Introduction. The major forms of control of finance exercised by Parliament are through the media of the Public Accounts Committee, and the Public Expenditure Committee, the latter having replaced the long-standing Select Committee on Estimates in 1971.

4. The Public Accounts Committee. Although theoretically appointed to exercise the *legal* aspect of control, the Committee has, in recent years, concentrated more on the elimination of waste, the encouragement of sound practices in estimating, contracting and financial administration generally and the need to obtain value for money, e.g. the inquiry into and the subsequent repayment of excess profits in the Ferranti Case. Its *formal functions* are:

(*a*) to audit the accounts and to guard the procedures and priorities of control by Parliament;
(*b*) to act as an outside audit on the propriety and honesty of departments' operations.

5. Importance of the Committee. The committee has achieved great esteem and effectiveness, although it has no executive power, and its examination of accounts is two years behind their presentation, and it has been the most important committee for controlling the executive for the following reasons.

(*a*) It has high political status being chaired traditionally by ex-ministerial Opposition chairmen.
(*b*) Its criticisms are highly respected in Whitehall, more from the aspect of their political repercussions than in the normal

auditing sense, particularly as civil service reputations are seen as being at stake in appearances before the committee.

(c) It is essentially concerned with efficiency rather than strict legal control and is regarded as a major check on bureaucratic mismanagement.

(d) Its work has led to direct improvements in government procedures, e.g. the practice of development contracting in government departments was introduced and still operates as a result of the Committee's criticisms of the previous practice, in 1968, between Bristol Siddley Engines and the Ministry of Aviation.

6. Criticism. Despite its considerable authority and achievements the machinery of the Committee is not appropriate for checking the efficiency of departments and the avoidance of waste. This is essentially a responsibility which must lie with the departments themselves and with the Treasury. In addition it is often difficult to distinguish the role of the Public Accounts Committee from that of the Expenditure Committee and in fact both committees have on occasions produced reports covering the same areas, e.g. the Expenditure Committee's Report on public investment in the private sector had shortly before been dealt with by the Public Accounts Committee.

PUBLIC EXPENDITURE COMMITTEE

7. Scrutiny of public expenditure and administration. To follow up the annual expenditure debate, the Select Committee on Procedure recommended that there should be instituted an Expenditure Committee empowered to effect more detailed scrutiny. The Committee, which was set up in early 1971, replaced the old Estimates Committee and has the power to investigate the whole field of public expenditure, unlike the Estimates Committee which was limited to that part specifically covered by the estimates. The new committee works through six functionally specialised sub-committees and one general co-ordinating sub-committee.

8. The old Estimates Committee. Although, since 1971, only of historical significance certain points relating to its functioning are worthy of mention. Implied in its formal terms of reference were the duties to determine whether administration was effective and economical, and critically to examine policy without challenging such policy. This seemingly contradictory latter point effectively meant that the committee could ask whether the financial demands of policy were reasonable and if the policy was effectively being carried out, but not whether such policy was in fact initially justified. The Expenditure Committee is not subject to this limitation.

The main achievements in broad terms of the Committee were improved costing in departments; better use of management techniques, and the establishment of the Fulton Committee. The Committee however suffered from the following limitations:

(a) amateurism and a reluctance to introduce subject specialisation;

(b) lack of planning in approach to inquiries;

(c) absence of specialised support staff—the Public Accounts Committee (P.A.C.) always commanded greater respect in the departments, being backed by the Exchequer and Audit departmental staff;

(d) inability to pinpoint individual responsibility as compared again with the P.A.C.;

(e) failure to follow up because of inadequate staff;

(f) failure to develop means of commenting on the forward expenditure programmes of the government.

9. The Select Committee on Expenditure. As compared with the Estimates Committee which it replaced the following points of importance emerge.

(a) One of its functions is to examine the annual expenditure White Papers (see **13–16**), thus putting it in a position to elucidate information on gaps and other deficiencies in such White Papers, and to discourage further deficiencies.

(b) Whereas the Estimates Committee was limited by the annual nature of the estimates the Expenditure Committee is able to examine forward projections of public expenditure, to question the basis of their preparation and to require justification by the departments of the priorities contained therein. It is thus a *policy* committee as opposed to the Estimates Committee.

NOTE: The Committee was described on its formation (*New Society*, 4th February, 1971) as "the custodian of this whole experiment in more open government". Its degree of success or otherwise thus determines to an extent the degree to which

Parliament and, ultimately, the public may participate in expenditure decision-making.

10. Structure and role of the Committee. Instead of just examining expenditure on the basis of annual departmental estimates placed before Parliament, the committee can investigate the government's spending commitments, question ministers on their policies underlying them, and report to Parliament on its enquiries.

The Committee consists of forty-nine members drawn from all parties, grouped into six sub-committees which examine specific fields of activity and have their reports discussed by the main committee. A steering · committee of fifteen members co-ordinates the work of the sub-committees. There is one sub-committee for each of the following areas of investigation:

(a) public expenditure (general);
(b) defence and external affairs;
(c) trade and industry;
(d) education and the arts;
(e) environment and the Home Office;
(f) employment and social services.

Each sub-committee consists of eight members and usually takes evidence in public. The sub-committees are serviced by expert staff.

NOTE: Important topics and subjects of reports produced to date by the Committee and its sub-committees include public money in the private sector, education and the arts, private practice in the national health service, urban transport planning, and, in 1978, the civil service (see VI, 27–28).

A PROPOSED TAXATION COMMITTEE

11. Nature of the proposal. The Select Committee on Procedure as long ago as 1967 suggested the establishment of a committee to examine proposals for new forms of taxation and for changes in the structure of existing taxes in advance of the budget. The basic idea was that such a committee should be a sub-committee of the Expenditure Committee and should study amongst other things the emphasis on indirect taxation, arguments in favour of subsidies as opposed to negative income tax, and the effects of allowances on the erosion of the tax base. The establishment of such a committee has been consistently opposed by the Treasury, though a strong case was put for the establishment of such a committee by Peter Jay (now British Ambassador to U.S.A.) when he was Economics Editor of *The Times*.

12. The case for taxation committee.

(a) The Treasury view that such a committee would be inconsistent with "the existing constitutional framework" is not relevant as the committee would be concerned with the long-term view and not on current short-term proposals, and thus would not impinge on the necessary confidentiality of taxation changes.

(b) "Many of the issues would be highly politically charged and political tension might arise within the Committee which would inhibit the objective examination of proposals. . . ." However this Treasury argument has not been advanced against the Expenditure Committee, and would in any case be offset as a result of its reports leading to better informed debates in the House.

(c) The Treasury objection that the Committee would stray into the field of policy formulation may be countered by techniques enabling the separation of analysis and decision-making, the latter in any case hardly being the province of a committee of this nature.

THE EXPENDITURE WHITE PAPERS

13. The concept. Both the Plowden Report on the Control of Public Expenditure (Cmnd. 1432, 1961) and the Report of the Select Committee on Procedure *Scrutiny of Public Expenditure and Administration* (1967) drew attention to the shortcomings of the traditional form of presentation of public expenditure policy. In response to the Plowden Report, White Papers on Public Expenditure appeared from 1963–9, though all essentially represented special products designed to meet particular situations, and the normal parliamentary business of dealing with public expenditure continued to be related to the annual supply estimates.

14. The Green Paper (1969): Public Expenditure—A New Presentation. It had become clear by the end of 1969 that the annual surveys were constituting the framework within which the government were taking major decisions on expenditure, and the

Green Paper recommended that there should be an annual White Paper showing the results of each year's public expenditure survey by the government. The presentation of the White Paper should be an integral part of the annual parliamentary financial cycle.

15. The White Papers. These have been produced annually since 1969 based on the annual "PESC" (Public Expenditure Survey Committee (*see* **21** below)) exercise. The White Papers contain figures for the preceding, the current, and four succeeding years, though of course after the first succeeding year the figures are only of a broad indicative nature. Expenditure is then broken down in four ways.

(*a*) By programme, e.g. defence, social services, debt interest.

(*b*) By spending authority, i.e. the branch of government concerned.

(*c*) By economic strategy. This shows the effect of state spending on the national income and expenditure in the economy, broken down into current and capital expenditure.

(*d*) By demand on output. This tries to work out the true effects of government spending on national demand.

NOTE: The figures have to be treated with caution as each figure is estimated on the basis of prices ruling when the estimate is made, and, as the figures are compiled over a period of months the use of different price bases at the time of rapid inflation makes the total of different types of expenditure meaningless. Criticisms of the approach are dealt with further below in relation to PESC.

16. Role of estimates. White Papers are supplementary to existing procedures, and the consideration in depth of actual policy remains a matter for separate presentation and debate on Supply Days, introduction of Green Papers, etc. The estimates thus retain their independent role in the context of the House's formal legal control.

PUBLIC EXPENDITURE MANAGEMENT

17. The official side. Having examined Parliament's role in relation to public expenditure it is necessary, in order to present a clear picture, to examine the major forms of organisation and process on the official side. It must be borne in mind however that the process of public expenditure is a joint process and it concerns essentially the Cabinet at the political level, and the Cabinet Office, the Treasury, and the Civil Service Department at the official level. In addition to the structure at the centre the question arises as to the relationship of the centre with the major departments.

18. Functions in the centre. The departmental structure at the centre is a combination of the Cabinet Office, the Treasury and the Civil Service Department (C.S.D.). These three organisations, headed by the holders of the top posts in the Home Civil Service may be conveniently regarded as a single group, though in practice the degree of their interrelationship varies according to changing political circumstances. The expenditure functions of these three bodies may be summarised as:

(*a*) the *Cabinet secretariat* which exercises a co-ordinating role;

(*b*) the *Civil Service Department* which is responsible for advising the Prime Minister on the machinery of government as well as being responsible for the civil service itself;

(*c*) the *Treasury* which is concerned with the management of the economy; home and overseas finance; fiscal policy; and co-ordination of economic policy.

19. The centre and the departments. The functions of the centre in relation to the departments are:

(*a*) central work on the departments' objectives and priorities known as *Programme Analysis and Review* (PAR);

(*b*) analysis of issues for the Cabinet by the Central Policy Review Staff;

(*c*) public expenditure allocation carried out by the Public Expenditure Survey Committee (PESC) of the Treasury through its public sector divisions;

(*d*) control of departmental manpower requirements by the C.S.D.

The role of the centre impinges on the role of departmental ministers in that decisions are taken which impose constraints on the departments; these constraints are determined by the Cabinet; and the centre must make sure that the departments comply with the constraints. This is a joint responsibility and the relationship should be, according to the Plowden Committee, "one of joint working together in a common enterprise; it should be considered not in terms of more or less independence of the departments from control by the Treasury, but rather in terms of getting the right balance and differentiation of function".

20. PAR and PESC. These are essentially related operations in a large overall process aimed at enabling the government to:

(*a*) create an overall policy for resource use;
(*b*) establish departmental objectives and priorities;
(*c*) establish a framework for allocation between departments;
(*d*) ensure departments keep within their allocations;
(*e*) provide an effective means of making day-to-day decisions within the overall strategy.

21. PESC. This is the principal means of inter-departmental co-ordination under Treasury chairmanship. PESC is responsible for the assessment of programmes and their implications for public expenditure as a whole against the background of medium-term economic analysis, and for producing the annual report for ministers on which basic decisions on public spending are taken, and on which the subsequent White Paper is founded.

22. Decision-making: programme analysis and review (PAR). The Treasury under the Chief Secretary is now responsible for managing the PAR programme. It has involved setting up machinery parallel to PESC in the form of the Programme Analysis and Review Committee (PARC) with a common chairman and overlapping membership.

The work of the committee is essentially concerned with establishing alternative ways of achieving given objectives; better measurement of the input of such activities; and better measurement of the outputs in order to enable more valid comparisons to be made. The PAR programme has had the following side effects:

(*a*) on *departments* where it requires trained and experienced staff;
(*b*) on *ministers* in that it requires them to submit important aspects of their departments' work for scrutiny;
(*c*) on the *Treasury* for providing the main stimulus behind the programme.

23. Some failings of the PESC system. In determining the public expenditure forecasts particular problems have become apparent which have led to difficulties in controlling public expenditure.

(a) Although the calculations involved indicate the volume of spending no system has been evolved whereby accurate long-range forecasts can be made.

(b) It works on the assumption that taxation policies will remain static and thus separates public spending decisions from tax decisions.

(c) The existence of unexpected contingencies cannot be allowed for.

THE TREASURY

24. The Treasury structure. The work of the Treasury is divided into four main sectors. At the head of the Department is a permanent secretary. Three of the divisions are headed by a second permanent secretary and the other by the Chief Economic Adviser.

(a) *The Chief Economic Adviser's Sector.* This consists of economists who deal with economic forecasting and the use of the Treasury's macro-economic model for the simulation of the effects on the economy of major economic policy options.

(b) *The Overseas Finance Sector.* This deals with international monetary policy, the financial aspects of E.E.C. membership, exchange control, reserve management, balance of payments, overseas aid, and export finance.

(c) *The Domestic Economy Sector.* This sector has two main areas of responsibility. Firstly, it has a close relationship with industry aimed at relating government policy effects with industrial decision-making. Secondly, it is concerned with counter-inflation policies, taxation policy, and monetary policy.

(d) *Public Services Sector.* This is responsible for control over public expenditure and the annual public expenditure survey.

NOTE: Co-ordination of the sectors is provided through the medium of a Central Unit, the unit also taking responsibility for areas of policy which transcend sector boundaries, e.g. budget preparation.

25. Treasury control. The Treasury fills an almost unique role amongst central finance departments in being the sole ministry of finance. Prior to the creation of the Civil Service Department it combined financial control with control over government personnel, and over civil service organisation and methods.

NOTE: The Treasury still retains an influential role in civil service matters (*see* VIII).

Treasury control is exercised through the media of co-ordination of financial policy (*see* **26–27**), co-ordination of economic policy (*see* **29–31**) and influence over the nationalised industries and the civil service (*see* **35**). It also holds a vital role in the whole decision-making process (*see* V).

26. Co-ordination of financial policy. This may be broken down into the following aspects.

(*a*) *The requirement of prior approval*. Departments are obliged to obtain Treasury approval of any variation in their activities that has a financial aspect. In general it is departmental practice to consult the Treasury during the planning stage of new activities and, while Treasury attention centres mainly on proposed new services, recurrent expenditure and services are only accorded freedom from Treasury control to the extent that the Treasury sees fit.

(*b*) *Criticism of new legislation and policy*. Although the requirement of prior approval (coupled with approval of estimates) is the foundation of the Treasury's power to co-ordinate financial policy, the Treasury possesses the further right of examining and criticising new policy proposals before they reach Cabinet level. Control of this nature is reinforced by the following:

(*i*) the Chancellor's power to delay Cabinet decisions until his officials have prepared a brief;

(*ii*) the usual practice of early consultation between departments and the Treasury;

(*iii*) the Cabinet rule that no proposals are circulated until the Chancellor's sanction has been obtained. This rule affords the Treasury an opportunity of pointing out financial consequences and thus enables it to act, in practice, as a staff agency advising departments on the formulation of policy.

(*c*) *Priorities in expenditure*. The annual review of departmental estimates is submitted to the Treasury before submission to

Parliament. The Chancellor, with the aid of the Treasury and in consultation with the ministers concerned, determines in advance the relative orders of magnitude which he proposes for different sections of government expenditure.

(d) *Annual review of estimates*. The detailed patterns of expenditure are reviewed in the annual estimates of expenditure. The Treasury, in addition to first examination of the estimates, also receives forward estimates from the departments. This provides it with an enlarged perspective from which the annual estimates may be regarded.

27. The importance of financial control. Treasury control operates as an effective safeguard against the misuse of executive powers, and provides an administrative balance against the powerful position of the executive under the British system of Cabinet government (*see* II). In particular, the following points should be noted.

(a) The requirement of prior approval does not mean automatic approval of the estimates, and neither does approval of the estimates dispense with prior approval. The requirement of prior approval involves a more detailed examination of proposed expenditure than does the estimates, and also relates to future expenditure.

(b) Although legally the Appropriation Act does not bind the departments to sub-heads and items in the original estimates, freedom is diminished by Treasury safeguards. Deviation from sub-heads is only permitted in the civil departments with Treasury approval, and the Treasury decides whether proposed deviations are of such significance as to require bringing to the notice of Parliament.

NOTE: The service departments have freedom to transfer items, but may transfer between sub-heads only with Treasury approval.

(c) The importance of Treasury control is emphasised by the weakness of parliamentary control. In compelling circumstances the executive can legally incur future expenditure not provided for in the Appropriation Act. The Treasury, however, is able to examine future implications of policy, and its approval is needed for activities involving contingent future liabilities. This involves interaction between Treasury and departmental officials.

(*d*) By reason of its scope, Treasury control tends to induce ministers to look beyond immediate problems.

(*e*) It provides valuable staff assistance to the departments with regard to the implications of future policy.

28. Ensuring economy. The traditional "housekeeping" functions of the Treasury are still exercised but "the trend is away from meticulous control of detail in favour of greater delegation to departments, combined with the use of methods which will enable the Treasury to satisfy itself that the standards of prudent housekeeping are being observed" (Sir Edward Bridges, *Treasury Control*, Stamp Memorial Lecture (London), 1950).

> NOTE: In this respect, there is a division of responsibility between the Treasury and departmental officials, and between the Treasury and the Expenditure and Public Accounts Committees.

29. Co-ordination of economic policy. The responsibility for the co-ordination of economic policy has fluctuated between various bodies during the twentieth century. The following stages can be noted.

(*a*) Before 1914. Responsibility rested with the Treasury with peripheral functions vested in such bodies as the Board of Trade.

(*b*) 1925. Responsibility was vested in a Cabinet Committee on Economic Research.

(*c*) 1930–9. Responsibility was vested in an Economic Advisory Council chaired by the Prime Minister. Despite its high rank the Council was limited by its lack of non-departmental duties.

(*d*) 1939–47. A Central Economic Information Service was set up within the Cabinet secretariat. This was divided in 1941 into the Central Statistical Office and the Economic Section.

(*e*) 1947–64. Economic policy responsibilities were returned to the Treasury in 1947. This period saw a marked reaction against physical control as a means of economic planning (*see* XII) and began a period of more direct Treasury control through monetary and fiscal means. The early 1960s, however, saw an attempt by the Tory Government to reduce the Treasury's absolute control, by establishing economic planning machinery, e.g. the National Economic Development Council and National Incomes Commission.

However, during the whole period the Treasury retained final responsibility for control of economic planning.

30. Treasury control. This was achieved through the following agencies:

(*a*) the Central Statistical Office, which provided factual information concerning economic growth.

(*b*) the Economic Section of the Treasury, which dealt with the study of economic problems.

(*c*) the two national economic groups of the Treasury, which undertook responsibility for economic forecasting and development of policies for economic growth.

> NOTE: The economic planning and co-ordinating functions were directly aided by the Treasury's direct responsibility for the budget and supervision of government expenditure.

31. The Department of Economic Affairs (D.E.A.). Prior to 1964 therefore various attempts had been made to control and co-ordinate economic policy. These took the form principally of advisory committees (before 1940), physical controls under non-departmental ministers (1940–7) and Treasury control (1947–64). In 1964 the D.E.A. was established with specific responsibility for economic policy.

32. Disadvantages of Treasury Control. Advocates of the D.E.A. pointed to the following defects in Treasury control.

(*a*) The Treasury was essentially economy-minded and consequently lacked the necessary approach for a planning department.

(*b*) Fiscal and monetary control were inadequate, and a more positive approach was needed which could only be achieved through the creation of a new department.

(*c*) The Treasury was overworked and lacked the necessary staff.

(*d*) The Chancellor of the Exchequer tended to leave too much influence over economic planning in the hands of the Treasury.

(*e*) There was a need to plan with regional disparities in mind and the Treasury was not suitable for this purpose.

33. Structure of the D.E.A. The D.E.A. had no executive responsibilities, being concerned principally with short- and long-term economic policy. It was staffed with a high concentration of economists, statisticians and industrialists, and headed by a Cabinet minister. It operated through five divisions, two for economic co-ordination, one for long-term economic planning, one for industrial policy and one for regional development. The divisions sought to co-ordinate the activities of the various economic departments, in particular the Treasury, the Board of Trade, the Ministries of Labour, Technology, Power, and Transport.

In addition it was responsible for the National Plan of 1965, and attempted to develop a prices and incomes policy through the National Board for Prices and Incomes. It also encouraged regional development through the creation of Development Councils in the regions.

34. Return to Treasury control. The Department of Economic Affairs was abolished in 1970 and the economic planning and co-ordination functions returned to the Treasury. The principal arguments in favour of the return to Treasury control were as follows.

(*a*) The Treasury's main concern is with financial policy and the Budget. As the Budget is a major economic weapon the Treasury should have responsibility for economic policy in general.

(*b*) As the Chancellor of the Exchequer raises revenue for the government, he should take the central place in the economic planning machinery.

(*c*) The absence of Treasury control would lead to irresponsible and financially unwise policies, and would result in friction between the D.E.A. and the Treasury.

(*d*) The Treasury has a special place in the machinery of government, with its power of direct influence over all departments. This position could not be matched by the D.E.A.

35. Other areas of Treasury control. These are as follows:

(*a*) *Nationalised industries*. The Treasury has involvement with the nationalised industries in so far as these depend on the Treasury for investment capital. In 1956 the government placed a restriction on the open market borrowing of the industries, with the result that the industries have become dependent on the Treasury for their capital projects.

(*b*) *Civil service*. (*See* VI.)

PROGRESS TEST 8

1. What is Parliament's role in public expenditure?   (2)

2. Explain the functions and importance of the Public Accounts Committee.   (4–6)

3. Explain the role of the Expenditure Committee and comment on how it differs from the old Estimates Committee. (8–10)

4. What is the case for a select committee on taxation?   (11–12)

5. Explain the nature of the Public Expenditure White Papers.   (13–16)

6. Explain the relationship on the official side of the control and the spending departments.   (17–19)

7. What is involved in PAR and PESC?   (20–23)

8. What is meant by Treasury control?   (25)

9. How does the Treasury exercise its responsibility for the co-ordination of financial policy? What is the importance of Treasury control?   (26, 27)

10. An experiment was made in setting up a Department of Economic Affairs. Explain the disadvantages and advantages of the D.E.A. as compared with Treasury control.   (31–33)

CHAPTER IX

Financial Administration in Local Government

INTRODUCTION

1. Aim of the chapter. It is not the purpose of this chapter to present a critique of the various forms of local government income, nor to examine the financial relationship between central and local government (*see* XII), but to examine the administrative aspects of the local government financial system (i.e. the internal aspects) for the following reasons:

(*a*) to complete the overall picture of public expenditure procedures by dealing with local matters, central financial procedure having been dealt with in VIII;

(*b*) to present a comparative view of local government and central government financial procedures;

(*c*) to consider the administrative structure of local government finance and its attendant problems, e.g. amateur/professional relationships, the divorce of spending functions and financial control functions.

2. Matters involved in local financial administration. These include the following:

(*a*) routine control functions;

(*b*) the provision of financial information in support of the management function of local authorities;

(*c*) control through integration of finance with policy objectives and their achievement, e.g. P.P.B. (*see* XVI,**11**);

(*d*) measurement of performance in financial terms.

3. Problems of traditional organisation. Finance being an integral, if not the central, factor in local administration, it is necessary to isolate those factors which are characteristic of local administration and which have a bearing on problems of financial administration. These may be stated in general terms as follows.

(*a*) The frequent failure of local administration to establish a clear division of respective responsibilities and authority between elected members and officials.

(*b*) The absence of central objectives in local administration and consequent diffuseness of purpose between the various individual factors constituting the administrative whole.

(*c*) The problem of measuring the effective performance of functions as a result of the interplay of social and economic factors in local administration. This factor, however, is often misused when utilised as a defence against allegations of inefficiency in local administration, and techniques and practices now exist which moderate this disadvantage, e.g. management by objectives.

(*d*) The existence, in the typical local government organisation, of an absence of effort towards a corporate whole together with absence of overall objectives.

(*e*) The lack of such checks as exist in business management to prevent individuals hiding their responsibilities behind various group entities, e.g. committees and departments.

(*f*) Departmentalism and its disadvantageous effects on establishing overall objectives, co-ordination, etc. (*see* VII).

(*g*) Lack of independent criticism from within as a result of the tendency to merge policy and administrative functions in the elected members and consequently to reduce the status of officers to mere agents without individual initiative.

INTEGRATION OF FINANCIAL ADMINISTRATION

4. Principles of integration. Dr. A. H. Marshall (in *Financial Administration in Local Government*, George Allen & Unwin, 1976) maintained that integration should be the guiding principle in local government financial organisation. In particular he stressed the following points.

(*a*) Financial administration should not be independent and an end in itself, but should be interwoven with the overall local authority administrative structure.

(*b*) Financial responsibility should not only be a function of the Treasurer's department and the Finance Committee but should be diffused throughout the whole authority.

(*c*) A single officer should be responsible for financial work.

Such work should be conceived of as machinery for servicing the whole of the authority and not merely a number of un-co-ordinated units varying in aim and under different control.

NOTE: This principle, of course, goes to the root of local government and transcends mere financial administration, revealing the need in local authorities as a whole for a spirit of corporate responsibility to be evolved, and for overall objectives to be established.

(*d*) At policy formulation level, finance should be conceived as one of a number of aspects, each of which must have proper consideration and not as a separate isolated factor.

5. Difficulties in achieving integration. Integration as a concept of organisation and procedure is made difficult in local government as a result of the following.

(*a*) The existence of departmentalism and inter-committee rivalry. This has resulted from local administration taking the attitude in the past that it is a form of federation of loosely related services, rather than one of subsidiaries working towards a collective whole.

(*b*) The concept of the relationship between member and officer and the domination of the professional by the amateur.

(*c*) The treatment of finance as a control function rather than as an administrative function. Although the control function is still of great importance in securing accountability for public funds, the underlying administrative aspects and contribution of finance to policy formation cannot be overrated.

(*d*) The absence of central policy units in many authorities responsible for co-ordinating otherwise effectively independent departments and establishing overall policy objectives towards which the functional departments should work.

6. The purposes of integration. The objects of integrating financial administration with the overall administrative context of local government are as follows:

(*a*) to diffuse financial responsibility throughout the authority;

(*b*) to enable effective setting of objectives and the measurement of the performance of such objectives;

(*c*) to exert a direct influence towards rationalisation in a local authority's structure by highlighting deficiencies in organisation and procedure;

(d) to engender the habit of co-operation, both in financial and non-financial fields.

BUDGETARY PROCEDURES

7. Introduction. A local authority budget differs from the central government Budget in the following ways.

(a) It is essentially a revenue-raising exercise, whereas the national Budget is both a revenue-raising exercise, and the operation of techniques of monetary and fiscal control. The latter thus goes well beyond the normal meaning attributed to budget.

(b) Although not always successful, a local authority is effectively required to balance its budget by equating income with expenditure. Balancing the budget has long since ceased to be a national requirement.

NOTE: Although individual local authority budgets are not treated as having an economic regulation effect, taken collectively the total of local spending may be regulated by the central government, or individual local authorities may effectively regard themselves as constrained by overall exhortations to economy, etc.

8. Capital and revenue expenditures. At the basis of local government financial procedure is the distinction between "capital" and "revenue" expenditure. These terms are difficult to define precisely, particularly as they may vary according to the size of the local authority, but in general the distinction may be taken as relating to the nature of the assets produced by the expenditure; i.e. capital expenditure results in permanent, long-term benefits, whereas revenue expenditure deals with matters of a temporary or recurrent nature. In practice, capital expenditure must be raised by borrowing, whereas revenue expenditure must be raised annually. Thus the distinction raises questions of incidence, interst rates, effect of capital charges on revenue expenditure, etc.

NOTE: This chapter is principally concerned with revenue expenditure and capital expenditure will be only generally approached (*see* **22–23**).

9. Functions of the revenue budget. The revenue budget has the following functions.

(a) It fixes the local rate and the purposes to which the income shall be applied.

(b) It assists policy-making functions by requiring annual review of services and an overall examination of the development of local functions. In practice, it is the only time the operation of the local authority is looked at as a whole.

(c) It represents a plan of action.

(d) It illustrates in financial terms the effect of policy options and changes.

(e) It provides a medium for ensuring that revenue is spent for the purposes provided (subject of course to "supplementaries", etc.).

(f) It provides a yardstick against which administrative performance can be judged, and encourages a methodical and responsible approach.

(g) It compels officers annually to review departmental aims and the means adopted for their fulfilment.

NOTE: Revenue budgets alter in form between local authorities and no statutory requirement as to form is established. However, the Institute of Municipal Treasurers and Accountants have introduced a standard form of accounts (*The Form of Published Accounts of Local Authorities*).

10. The local budget process. The traditional method of local authority budgeting involved a comparatively short time span, commencing in the autumn, when the service committees prepared their estimates, and finishing with the final precept or rate-fixing meeting of the council in February or March. The change to the corporate management approach has meant that most authorities operate over the whole year, and involves a continuous interaction between the roles of elected members, officers, the council as a whole, the policy and resources committee, and the service or programme committees. The process may be broken down into stages and the particular functions of different elements of the authority analysed as follows.

11. Preparation stage. This runs from February to April and involves the preparation of a "guidelines report" and updated structure plan by the *officers* which is submitted to the *policy and* *resources committee*, which in turn submits them to the *council* and to the *service committees*.

12. Guidelines stage. During this stage, which runs between April and July, the *council* ratifies the structure plan which is submitted to the *service committees* to consider its implications, which are supported by the *officers*. The reports of the committees are then submitted to the *council* through the *policy and resources committee* and future strategy is finalised.

13. Target stage. Between July and November the *service committees* apply in detail the council's decided strategy to service policies and options. At the same time the *officers* prepare capital programmes which are submitted to the service committees, who in turn report both on these programmes and on the operation of council strategy to the *policy and resources committee* which in turn reports back to the *council* which then establishes the financial targets.

14. Budget stage. Between November and March revenue programmes are prepared by the *officers*. The *committees* prepare capital and revenue programmes, and these programmes are summarised by the *policy and resources committee* which reports to the council. The *council* then fixes the rate.

THE POLICY AND RESOURCES COMMITTEE

15. Traditional position. Prior to the reorganisation effected in most authorities as a result of the Bains Report (*see* V, **20** and XVII, **19–25**), the major horizontal committee was the finance committee, particularly where no other formal means of co-ordination had been adopted. Its advantageous position resulted from two factors.

(*a*) It had knowledge of the overall financial position and requirements of the local authority.

(*b*) Being non-functional, it was better placed to take an overall and detached view of the authority's spending activities.

In addition where an authority was politically organised the council was in a position which made it difficult to override the views of the committee. On the other hand difficulty was caused by the inability to demarcate adequately between matters of policy and matters of finance, e.g. where the finance committee was required to consider the financial implications of a new service or the extension of an existing service.

16. The post-Bains position. The establishment of a central policy and resources committee, supported by resource sub-committees in respect of finance, land, and personnel, often together with a performance review committee, now means that a corporate approach may be established in respect of policy and finance matters. This position is achieved as:

(a) the policy and resources committee is a key structure in recommending policy;

(b) the reports of committees on the financial implications of the overall council strategy and their capital and revenue programme proposals are filtered through the policy and resources committee before submission to the council;

(c) the traditional function of routine financial control is exercised by the finance and other resource sub-committees and is only brought together with policy implications at policy and resources committee level;

(d) the composition of the policy and resources committee, invariably comprising the major committee chairmen, enables effective control and co-ordination to be exercised at this level.

17. Its similarity with Treasury control. The functions of the finance committee have been compared with those of Treasury control as defined by the Select Committee on Estimates, 1957–8, which are as follows:

(a) deciding on total expenditure;

(b) securing a proper balance between services;

(c) securing a proper balance of expenditure within services;

(d) helping determine expenditure on individual policies and services.

NOTE: Treasury control in fact goes beyond these functions and is facilitated by the hierarchical position occupied by the Treasury in the central government structure, a position not likely to be equalled by a finance committee.

THE FINANCE DEPARTMENT

18. Importance. The finance (or treasurer's) department of a local authority occupies a central position in the departmental structure for the following reasons.

(*a*) It is in a unique position to counteract the forces of departmentalism.

(*b*) It can be organised in such a way as to avoid the obsession with detail which is such a characteristic of committee level operations.

19. Its relationship with the spending departments. It is usual for there to be regular collaboration and consultation between the finance department and the individual operational departments. This manifests itself particularly in the drawing up of the estimates with discussions taking place on new items of expenditure and alterations to existing items between departmental and finance department officials. In addition, it will be the responsibility of the finance department to interpret the implications of the finance committee's views to the departments.

> NOTE: The influence of the finance department on the spending committees and departments is difficult to quantify owing to the interplay of such factors as relative strengths of committees and departments, the political structure of the authority, tradition, personalities of chairmen, etc.

One vital factor in the finance department's role is the annual *Report* of the treasurer to the finance committee, though again its importance varies among local authorities according to the importance of various intangible factors. The *Report* itself is of considerable significance in that it sets out such matters as the state of the local authority's working balances, its reserves, renewals and capital funds, changes expected in the future operations of the authority and such matters as trends in costs, etc.

BUDGETARY CONTROL

20. Nature of budgetary control. Traditionally, the finance department exercises routine "after the event" control, the more rigorous checking being a function of the spending departments. Its function will also be affected by standing orders which may permit the treasurer to authorise variations due to unexpected factors, e.g. pay awards, and which may restrict "virement", i.e. changes of expenditure between items. This latter may be permitted where a saving on one item is due to economy, as opposed to representing a mere fortuitous gain.

NOTE: The increase of computerisation both facilitates budgetary control in local authorities and enables the use of new forms of such control; e.g. it permits an accounting system based on control of commitments rather than of expenditures.

21. P.P.B. (*see* XVI, **11**). The importance of the development of the use of P.P.B. in local government is as follows.

(*a*) It facilitates the establishment of a system of overall objectives with subsidiary departmental and committee objectives. It consequently cuts across departmental factors and subordinates these to the goals of the authority as a whole.

(*b*) It requires, of necessity, long-term policy formulation and consideration on an overall basis of related services.

(*c*) It requires supplementation of the programmed budget by sub-objectives, and techniques for the measurement of performance.

(*d*) It may contribute accordingly to the establishment of central research and statistical units, e.g., as in the G.L.C.

(*e*) It avoids the traditional conceptual difference between capital and revenue proposals.

(*f*) It places emphasis on long-term financial strategy rather than the present annual approach.

CAPITAL EXPENDITURE

22. Capital expenditure programmes. Because of their large and long-term effects, it is vital that a local authority has adequate machinery for the review of capital expenditure proposals. In general, the procedure for approval of capital commitments is as follows.

(*a*) The project is scrutinised when it is included in the long-term capital programme. The programme is of great importance, as it enables decisions to be taken on such matters as priorities, effects on the revenue budget, forward planning, etc.

(*b*) The programme is submitted to the council.

(*c*) Central government sanction must be sought (*see* XII).

23. Form of the long-term programme. This is a matter which has been facilitated in certain authorities by the use of O.R. techniques (*see* XVI). Essentially the programme must contain a long-term projection (three to five years), classification of schemes put forward, annual charges and running costs, as these will affect future revenue budgets, and reports of the officers concerned pointing out the effects of the capital programme on the overall finances and objectives of the authority.

CONCLUSIONS

24. Views of the Maud Committee on Management. The Committee favoured the establishment of a centralised management board (*see* XVII) which, amongst other matters, would assume financial responsibilities. This proposal was opposed by the Institute of Municipal Treasurers and Accountants, which not only felt that financial control would be effectively reduced, but also mentioned the following points.

(*a*) Financial administration and control should be independent of the main spending elements in the local authority.

(*b*) Financial administration and control should be the responsibility of the treasurer, who should have a direct right of communication to all management levels.

(*c*) The treasurer, should continue to be under a public obligation to maintain the integrity and openness of the control system.

25. Comparison with central government. In making comparisons between central and local financial administration, the following factors must be borne in mind:

(*a*) the much greater diversity exhibited in local systems;

(*b*) the much greater number of intangible factors in local matters;

(*c*) the greater influence of officials in the central structure;

(*d*) the much greater detailed control exercised by local elected representatives;

(*e*) the absence of a local body with the powers of the Treasury.

PROGRESS TEST 9

1. What problems were commonly involved in traditional local authority financial organisation?   **(3)**

2. What are the "principles of integration" laid down by Dr. A. H. Marshall? What are the objects of such integration? **(4, 6)**

3. Describe the difficulties in achieving integration. **(5)**

4. Compare the budgetary procedure of a local authority with that of the central government. **(7)**

5. Distinguish between capital and revenue expenditure. What are the functions of the revenue budget? **(8, 9)**

6. Outline the budgetary process in local authorities. **(10–14)**

7. What are the functions and relations of the policy and resources committee? **(15–16)**

8. How do the functions of the policy and resources committee resemble Treasury control? **(17)**

9. What are the functions and relations of the Finance Department? **(18–19)**

10. What is involved in budgetary control in a local authority? **(20–21)**

CHAPTER X

Planning

INTRODUCTION

1. A definition of planning. There has always been a tendency to give planning emotive connotations, particularly in the context of the controversy between individualism and collectivism. This approach tends to obscure the true meaning and purpose of the planning process. It is thus necessary objectively to define planning, and to determine the goals and criteria obtaining therein.

Planning has been defined as "that activity that concerns itself with proposals for the future, with the evaluation of alternative proposals, and with the methods by which these proposals may be achieved" (H. A. Simon, D. W. Smithburg and V. A. Thompson, *Public Administration*, Alfred Knopf, 1967). Planning is thus concerned with future human behaviour and involves both the following.

    (*a*) *Ultimate activities*. Those anticipated if a plan is carried out.
    (*b*) *Intermediate activities*. Those required to carry out the plan.

2. The reasons for planning. Planning is indispensable to the administrative process as any decision and consequent activities carried out to achieve the objectives of that decision will limit the range of choices available to the administrator in future owing to the limited nature of resources. It is thus necessary whenever the execution of policy involves "sunk costs".

3. Planning goals. The traditional administrative theory of the distinction between policy and administration, i.e. between the formation of the plan and its execution is not practicable in planning for the following reasons.

    (*a*) By their political connections and involvement, planning bodies can rarely be neutral and therefore underlying any long-range planning objectives of a government will be assumptions as to what are the desirable goals to be achieved.

(*b*) Short-term goals are probably less overtly political, though they must of course work within the framework of the long-term plan.

(*c*) The executive organs are involved in planning in both their function as supplier of the basic material upon which the plan is based and in their function of "planning for planning", i.e. establishing the organisational framework necessary for implementation of a plan.

A basic requirement in planning is that of co-ordination in order that contradiction of goals between various groups involved in the plan is avoided. Rational co-ordination in turn can only be achieved if there is some overriding goal to which all the groups are working. In a democracy the process of co-ordination is made more difficult, and of necessity becomes a political function which must be set against dominant social goals.

4. Implementation of goals. In order to be effective, planning must be concerned not only with materialistic ends but also with human behaviour which may inhibit the achievement of the goals. Such planning goals must therefore attempt to rationalise and account for the following.

(*a*) *Resistance to goals*. Resistance may be expressed overtly or, more commonly, implicitly, and may be effected by inertia, community or personal values, self-interest or dislike of subordination.

(*b*) *Dynamics of planning*. An operable plan must account for elements which are not directly under the influence of the plan and how these external factors may affect achievement of the plan's goals. This necessity arises as no plan can be comprehensive and must therefore seek some form of evaluation of non-planned factors.

5. Organisation for planning. In general terms, planning may take place through specialised planning units or through units of government which at the same time perform other functions. In the first place, however, whichever type of unit is utilised, it is necessary that planning should take place at a level where there is responsibility for the achievement of some overriding and unitary social policy, and thus there is a natural tendency, as government activities become more complex, for the level of integration of planning to rise in the administrative structure.

The advantages of non-functional planning units are as follows:

(a) they secure proper attention to research;

(b) they are not dominated by political objectives and controversies outside the scope of the plan;

(c) they will generally be concerned with long-range aspects of a plan with shorter-range planning taking place through the administrative process;

(d) pressure of day-to-day administration will not be present to divert attention from long-range problems. When a planning unit is contained in a functional organisation there is a tendency for resistance to the planning unit to occur, and such resistance may be in fact encouraged as the planning unit relieves the rest of the organisation from long-term responsibilities.

POLITICAL CONSEQUENCES OF ECONOMIC PLANNING

6. Fundamental difficulties. Economic planning, of necessity, requires the granting of considerable executive discretion in order to facilitate immediate response to economic contingencies. Continual reference to political control will thus inhibit the effective implementation of a plan. There thus arises the basic problem of resolving the need for executive discretion with adequate political surveillance. This in turn is made difficult by the following:

(a) the inadequacy of annual budgets to achieve such political control;

(b) weak control of public expenditure (but *see* VIII).

7. Political problems in planning. Political problems arise as a result of the long-term commitments involved in planning. These problems may be classified as follows.

(a) The binding nature of planning on future governments. Although commitments undertaken are not legally binding they may be *de facto* binding owing to a high degree of "sunk costs" and the rigidity or complexity of a plan.

(b) The undertaking of commitments over a period of time must be reconciled with the need to make such plans democratically responsive to changes in public opinion.

(c) Freedom in operating and modifying the plan accorded to

governments, ministers, administrators, etc., decreases proportionately the thorough-going nature of a plan.

(*d*) The budgetary process is too cumbersome for short-term policy responsiveness, and too limited in scope for long-term planning.

(*e*) There is a need to develop effective means of financial accountability and to prevent side-stepping of control exercised through the budgetary process.

(*f*) There is a danger that a gap may develop between the controllers of a plan and the operators, and that what are effectively political value judgments may be concealed by technical jargon.

(*g*) There has been a tendency to transfer planning functions to *ad hoc* bodies outside the sphere of ministerial responsibility. This transfer of power gives rise to problems of responsibility. The older institutions tended to be subordinate, peripheral or specialised bodies and within the direct control or influence of a minister. The new bodies present problems owing to the central role of planning in the government process and, as they tend to fall outside direct control, there is a need for the creation of extra-parliamentary safeguards.

(*h*) Promotion of economic growth is one of the prime influences on electoral opinion and therefore is the most political activity of government. There is thus the need to reconcile the role of public opinion with the need to take the unpopular decisions which planning necessarily involves.

MANAGEMENT OF THE BRITISH ECONOMY

8. The reasons for management. The great development in management of the economy and planning by the government may be attributed to a collection of non-political factors, in particular the following:

(*a*) the impact of the "Keynesian revolution" and the realisation that the maintenance of full employment is not secured by leaving the economy to the interplay of free market forces;

(*b*) the influence of the White Paper of 1944 and its emphasis on the social and economic responsibilities for the maintenance of full employment;

(*c*) the change in emphasis of the role of government;

(*d*) the growth of public expenditure and the realisation of its decisive effect on economic growth and the direction such growth should take.

9. The machinery for management. No coherent and co-ordinated approach has been made to the machinery of planning and economy co-ordination. There has been recourse to the conferment of new duties on old ministries, e.g. the old Board of Trade; the creation of new ministries, e.g. the short-lived Department of Economic Affairs; and the use of *ad hoc* agencies, e.g. Regional Planning Boards.

10. Development of machinery from 1945–64. By the end of the War economic planning had become a central political issue, but the problem of establishing permanent machinery had not been solved. The major developments were as follows.

(*a*) *1945–51*. The Labour Government made piecemeal attempts to establish central planning machinery. Initially there was created a Ministry of Economic Affairs and a Central Economic Planning Staff (C.E.P.S.) for giving information and advice. In support, both the Central Statistical Office (C.S.O.) and the Economic Section of the Cabinet (E.S.C.) were strengthened. However, this seemingly impressive force was largely concerned with the production of planning documents in the form of surveys. In 1947, the Ministry of Economic Affairs was wound up, and both the C.E.P.S. and responsibility for economic affairs were taken into the Treasury, which is not a suitable vehicle for long-term economic planning. In turn the C.E.P.S. was abolished in 1951, and in 1953 the Treasury absorbed the E.S.C.

Thus, in 1951, the only planning mechanism was an Economic Planning Board (E.P.B.) which was largely a toothless institution and, despite its being the major consultative committee on economic policy, it was not a central planning agency.

(*b*) *Developments in the early 1960s*. The Tory administrations during the 1950s did not extend central planning machinery and no change in attitude was noticeable until the beginning of the 1960s. The new approach was heralded by Mr Selwyn Lloyd in a parliamentary statement of 26th July 1961 in which he called for a more purposeful approach than that of the E.P.B., etc., with surveys over five-year periods, involving both sides of industry with the government in "the task of relating plans to the resources likely to be available".

(c) *Main suggestions*. The new approach gave rise to two principal suggestions as to the means of achieving these objectives, namely:

(i) the establishment of an independent planning body charged with the production of economic forecasts and projections;

(ii) a two-tier body with the top tier making policy and consisting of representatives of employers, unions, "outsiders", etc., and with a lower tier consisting of an office of experts.

(d) *The National Economic Development Council (N.E.D.C.)*. The latter approach was adopted, and manifested itself in the establishment of the N.E.D.C. This body was essentially advisory but had considerable powers of influence. It was assisted by a full-time office (N.E.D.O.) and had the duty of examining the development plans of the main industries in the private sector, and in the light of such examination studies would be prepared for the Council's examination.

N.E.D.C. consisted of six employers' representatives, six union representatives, two nationalised industries representatives, two academics, three ministers, and a director.

(e) *N.E.D.O.* The National Economic Development Office was divided into two main divisions. One dealt with a study of general economic issues and the other with problems and programmes of individual industries and sectors of the economy.

(f) *Economic Development Committees*. "Little Neddies" were created in 1963 to provide consultative machinery with the individual industries, on the assumption that by involving industry in national planning greater co-operation, etc., could be achieved. The machinery was based to an extent on that in operation in France (*see* XVIII).

11. Developments under the Labour Government, 1964–70. The essence of Labour Government alterations to the planning machinery was to provide a stronger and more authoritative form of planning. The Department of Economic Affairs was created with "responsibility for the management of the national economy as a whole". For this purpose the Department of Economic Affairs was divided into three groups, namely, Economic Planning and Public Expenditure, Regional Planning and Industrial Policies, and Prices and Incomes. The Department, however, suffered from the following defects which blunted its effect:

(a) poor relations with the Treasury existed owing to a clash of roles;

(b) recurrent economic crises strengthened the Treasury's hand against the Department of Economic Affairs;

(c) the National Plan which it produced soon proved to be obsolete and lacked any concrete programme, consisting as it did only of a general statement of objectives.

The Department of Economic Affairs was abolished by the Conservative Government in 1970.

12. The need for a planning agency. The desirability of a single central planning and co-ordinating agency is questioned by the experience of the Department of Economic Affairs. In favour of a similiar body are the following points.

(a) Planning depends essentially on the effective encouragement of economic growth, and how successful this is politically. These intertwined responsibilities can be more effectively carried out by a single agency.

(b) There is a vital need for a central department concerned with projecting and co-ordinating functions.

(c) The Treasury is inadequate for the carrying out of such functions (see VIII).

Against such an agency are the following points:

(d) The difficulty of reconciling the British preference for indicative as opposed to command planning with the creation of a strong authoritative central agency.

(e) The difficulty of creating a sufficiently high-ranking department, whilst at the same time giving adequate power to the individual departments.

13. Developments since 1970. Following the demise of the D.E.A. in 1970 the whole responsibility for finance and economic affairs returned to the Treasury, and, in the context of planning, the Chief Economic Adviser's section is responsible for economic forecasting, while the Domestic Economy Sector covers such matters as counter-inflation policies, taxation policy, etc. Other features in economic planning during this period have been as follows.

(a) Working parties were established in 1972, and still operated in 1978 on an *ad hoc* basis, with representatives from the government, the T.U.C. the C.B.I. and N.E.D.O. to draw up outline policies for pay and prices.

(b) In 1973 a Price Commission and a Pay Board were established.

(c) The Pay Board was abolished in 1974 on the establishment of the "Social Contract".

(d) The Industry Act 1975 provided for the establishment of a new body, the National Enterprise Board, to take over the government's shareholdings in private industry and with power to make new investments in the private sector. In addition a series of planning agreements were made between individual enterprises and the State.

(e) In 1975 the Government White Paper, *An Approach to Industrial Strategy* was published, the main effects being to firmly entrench planning with the Treasury and the Department of Industry, and to create a number of N.E.D.O. working parties for particular industries.

PROBLEMS OF PLANNING RESPONSIBILITY

14. Indicative planning. Planning in a liberal democracy such as Britain tends to be indicative, i.e. framework and objectives are worked out as guides and not as enforceable goals as in, for instance, the U.S.S.R. (*see* XVIII). Conditions in such a democracy involve the interaction of government authority with "pressure group" politics, and with areas outside the direct command of government which may, however, be influenced by controls (physical, fiscal, etc.). Indicative planning thus requires that these outside interest groups actively participate and will be involved in discussion, bargaining, etc., in order that they may become involved with the decision-makers in the carrying out of the plan.

15. The extent of ministerial control. The strong position of the executive under the British system of Cabinet government is made acceptable and consensus is created by the traditions of responsible and representative government. Ultimately, responsibility to the electorate and to public opinion is the key to democratic control of government. But planning institutions which fall outside direct ministerial control give rise to certain problems within this framework. In particular, there arises a clash between the following:

(a) the need for government involvement, e.g. in N.E.D.C., in order to secure union and employer co-operation;

(b) the desirability of freedom from direct government control. Any such advantages accruing (e.g. co-operation in planning) must be set against the government's ultimate responsibility to the electorate and the impossibility, therefore, of its being bound by the recommendations of such bodies.

NOTE: Further difficulty is occasioned in attempting to define the boundaries of ministerial responsibility for such matters as a National Plan. The extent to which ministers are responsible for securing the ends of the Plan and for micro-factors within the Plan is difficult to define and difficult to fit within existing concepts of ministerial responsibility.

16. Suggested reforms. The following points should be noted.

(a) *The role of Parliament.* Legislation plays comparatively little part in national planning and thus the strengthening of Parliament's critical function is most desirable (*see* II).

(b) *Committees.* Linked with (a) is the need to extend the role of the committee system (*see* II).

(c) *Increased publicity.*

17. Planning and interest groups. Possibly the main political solution to the problem of responsibility and planning is the strengthening of interest groups and the machinery through which they may express their views. A case may be argued for strong constitutional and formalised interest group machinery, such as the French Economic and Social Council which provides a forum for discussion and resolution of conflicts. Other suggestions which have been put forward include the conversion of the House of Lords into an Industrial Second Chamber. It is important, however, that the strength of parliamentary government is not debased in any attempt to elevate the status of interest groups. In particular, the interest group system suffers from certain substantial disadvantages in relation to Parliament, namely:

(a) it cannot guarantee the proper representation of all interests;

(*b*) it cannot provide a system of government in a liberal democracy;

(*c*) it cannot provide a background of general and moral issues and beliefs essential to democracy.

18. The interrelation of physical and social planning. The following points should be noted.

(*a*) *Physical plans.* The first compulsory and national physical planning policy was embodied in the Town and Country Planning Act 1947, and the New Towns Act of the preceding year. These established an elaborate apparatus of physical planning controls. These were not, however, related to vital economic questions, such as the economic costs of physical planning in limiting urban growth, accommodation of overspill and construction of new towns. These questions were rarely dealt with in the context of the relation of the cost of economic resources to the benefits accruing. It was not until the later 1950s and the 1960s that it became common to relate physical planning to underlying economic and social data.

(*b*) *Social planning.* Prior to 1939 there was a growing government responsibility for public welfare. This manifested itself in the growing public social sector after the War and in government involvement in what had hitherto been matters of private, or peripherally public, concern.

(*c*) *Multi-disciplinary planning.* The first multi-disciplinary planning exercises have now taken place, though generally on a regional basis. This development has been brought about by the following:

(*i*) dissatisfaction with the planning achievements of the 1950s;

(*ii*) the effects of the population explosion and transport revolution;

(*iii*) the development in economic planning and its emphasis on growth;

(*iv*) the political stimulus to regional policy.

REGIONAL PLANNING

19. Introduction. In Great Britain and Western Europe in general, regional planning has primarily been conceived of at national level, e.g. the Distribution of Industry Acts. In general there has been a failure to treat regions as other than spots of localised unemployment, and a reluctance to treat them as "polarised integrated wholes" (J. R. Boudeville, *Problems of Regional Economic Planning*, Edinburgh University Press, 1966). Regions have thus been treated as areas which would spontaneously develop as action was taken to stimulate the economy as a whole. This policy for spontaneous development has been proved inadequate and the necessity of treating regions as independent problems has been highlighted, e.g. by long-term unemployment in the North-East. Consequently, decentralised regional planning becomes necessary and stems either from a federal concept of the state, or from some type of administrative deconcentration.

20. The need for regional policy. The following aspects should be noted.

(*a*) *Political.* Apart from questions of governments' electoral self-interest, questions of separatist movements affecting the cohesion of the state may arise through neglect of regional disparities, e.g. as in Belgium between Walloon and Flemish areas.

(*b*) *Social.* This factor will include such matters as redistribution of income, preservation of cultural backgrounds, equalising of opportunity, etc.

(*c*) *Economic.* This factor has three main parts:

(*i*) a recognition of the inadequacy of economic forces to operate satisfactorily in location of industry matters;

(*ii*) the incompatability of growth and idle resources;

(*iii*) the fact that inflation avoidance and growth encouragement are only effective if wide regional unemployment disparaties are avoided.

21. Regional policy in the 1960s. This may be stated briefly as follows:

(*a*) The Local Employment Act 1960 (as amended and strengthened in 1963) which replaced the old development area concept with a more flexible system of development districts;

(*b*) White Papers of 1963 on Central Scotland and on North-East England which provided the first step towards effective regional planning;

(*c*) The Industrial Development Act 1966 which replaced the development districts with new developing areas;

(*d*) increased use of controls, for example the Control of Office and Industrial Development Act 1965;

(*e*) grants, loans and financial inducements.

22. Regional Policy in the 1970s. Regional policy in the 1970s has shown little substantial advance. The main forms of regional policy involve the operation of inducements through the use of allowances and grants, in particular regional development grants introduced by the Industry Act 1972. These are administered through four Regional Development Grant Offices headed by an Assistant Secretary, and are payable only in assisted areas, but are available for buildings as well as new machinery or plant, but subject to central directions given by the Department of Industry.

Backing up the policy of inducements is the compulsive nature of Industrial Development Certificates which have to be obtained for industrial development above certain limits outside the assisted areas.

23. The system and purpose of regional planning. England was divided into eight planning regions by the Labour Government of 1964–70. Within each region there is a Regional Economic Council and a Regional Economic Planning Board. The Councils are representative institutions (though not elected) and the Boards are made up of civil servants.

The purpose of the machinery has been described by the Secretary of State as being "to provide effective machinery for regional economic planning . . . (and) for economic development. The Economic Planning Councils will be concerned with broad strategy on regional development and the best use of the region's resources . . . the Economic Planning Boards will provide machinery for co-ordinating the work of government departments concerned with regional planning and development, and their creation will not affect the existing powers and responsibilities of local authorities or existing ministerial responsibilities" (*Hansard*, 10th December 1964).

The initial problem will be to provide a regional strategy within which more detailed regional planning may then take place.

24. The functions of regional planning. These are as follows:

(*a*) to provide the basic cost and benefit data and analysis upon which regional planning policies may be based;

(*b*) to forecast a region's future pattern of development;

(c) to provide a plan for such matters as growth areas, the interrelation of the private sector, the need for investment, social capital, etc.

25. Problems of regional planning machinery. The following points should be noted:

(a) the need to establish the appropriate level and degree of democratic control and responsibility;

(b) co-ordination between central and regional authorities;

(c) the question of what machinery is appropriate.

26. The appropriate machinery. In general terms, regional planning machinery may take one of the following forms.

(a) Advisory bodies without executive responsibilities such as the present British system. In this case, the regional machinery merely advises and supplies data and recommendations upon which the central government may or may not act. Although this system has the advantage that reports may be made without the inhibitions which commitment to firm recommendations would have, it suffers from the disadvantage that, in general, reports never receive either the government or public attention which they might otherwise achieve.

(b) Executive bodies. The creation of such bodies would, however, pose certain problems:

(i) their effectiveness would depend largely on the provision of an independent source of finance;

(ii) problems of co-ordination both with government and other regional policy would arise;

(iii) such a body would of necessity be required to be democratically elected.

(c) Mandatory plans without executive capacity. This would involve the government in being bound by regionally prepared plans without the regional authorities themselves having executive capacity. This would imply, however, a degree of compulsion which governments would generally be unwilling to undertake, as well as giving rise to substantial problems of co-ordination.

PROGRESS TEST 10

1. What is meant by "planning"? What are the reasons for planning? **(1, 2)**

2. Consider the meaning and implementation of "planning goals". (**3, 4**)

3. How may organisation for planning be achieved? (**5**)

4. What are the fundamental *political* difficulties and problems of economic planning? (**6, 7**)

5. What are the reasons for government management of the economy? How was such management organised from 1945 to 1964? (**8, 10**)

6. What developments took place in the machinery during 1964–70? (**11**)

7. Consider the desirability of a single planning agency. (**12**)

8. Consider the major problems in planning responsibility. What reforms could be made? (**14–16**)

9. Consider the interrelations of planning and interest groups. (**17**)

10. How are physical and social planning interrelated? (**18**)

11. Why is regional planning needed? What was British policy in this field during the 1960s? (**19–23**)

12. What are the functions and problems of regional planning? (**24, 25**)

13. Consider the possible forms of appropriate machinery for regional planning. (**26**)

CHAPTER XI

Decentralisation and Regionalism

INTRODUCTION AND HISTORICAL BACKGROUND

1. Definitions. The following definitions should be noted.

(*a*) *Decentralisation*. This may be treated as a general term signifying the removal of functions from the centre, and may be either functional or geographical. Functional decentralisation is dealt with by various *ad hoc* authorities (*see* **25–28**). Geographical decentralisation consists of devolution to one of the following:

(*i*) bureaucratically controlled outposts of central government;

(*ii*) democratically elected authorities.

(*b*) *Deconcentration*. Method (*a*) (*i*) may be more conveniently termed administrative deconcentration.

(*c*) *Regionalism*. Decentralisation of decision-taking powers generally favours large regional areas, and may consist in the conferment of functions on either bureaucratically appointed or democratically elected bodies covering areas wider than those at present governed by local authorities.

2. The need for decentralisation. Some measure of decentralisation becomes necessary for the following reasons:

(*a*) the increasing complexity of government functions;

(*b*) the need to delegate information-collecting functions and decision-taking responsibilities in order to achieve greater efficiency;

(*c*) applying general policies and standards to local situations where the size of area and population served by an administrative system is large constitutes a major problem.

NOTE: The region is generally regarded as the most convenient area for achievement of the above aims, but as yet regional authorities are entirely bureaucratic deconcentrations of central government. The term "region" is however open to

some controversy in definition, e.g. between the planning regions and the "city regions" mentioned in the Senior memoran-
dum of dissent to the *Redcliffe-Maud Report* (*see* **18**).

3. Regional authorities. In determining the structure of regional
decentralised authorities three main problems arise, namely:

(*a*) definition of the areas of the authorities;
(*b*) the amount of decision-making authority to be delegated;
(*c*) the machinery for the co-ordination of the various
authorities.

> NOTE: In addition, two major areas which have to be settled
> for the purpose of efficiency of regional machinery are standard-
> isation of areas and standardisation of delegated powers (*see*
> **10**).

4. Background to historical development. There has been a
marked tendency for the regions adopted to vary according to
what is considered to be the optimum catchment area of the
particular decentralised function. However, in order to achieve
co-ordination and to enable these authorities to work coherently
towards an overall aim, it is necessary for the development of
common boundaries. This has been emphasised by the development of regional economic and environmental planning, and failure to achieve standardisation results in weakness at regional level
and confusion of co-ordination from the centre. The various
attempts at regional standardised patterns are described below.

5. 1939–45. England was divided into ten regions, each under a
commissioner. This was purely a response to the needs of wartime planning and ended in 1945. There was general antipathy
from local authorities towards this prefectorial system of government.

> NOTE: "Prefectorial type of regional co-ordination invariably
> creates tensions in a democratic polity, particularly where a
> high value is placed on the institutions of democratic local
> government" (James Fosler, "Centralisation and Decentralisa-
> tion", *International Encyclopaedia of the Social Sciences*,
> 1972).

6. Post-war period. During the post-war reconstruction period
the regional agencies of ministries were continued, e.g. in 1946
the Ministry of Health set up Regional Production Committees to

assist local authorities in conjunction with the Regional Building Committees. In 1946 the Treasury devised standard regions to prevent the random growth of regional agencies. Departments were obliged to comply with these unless they could produce good reasons for not so doing. Although these standard regions did not apply to *ad hoc* authorities, they operated as a catalyst for bringing together senior regional officials in a series of co-ordinating committees.

7. 1950s. There was a reaction against regional machinery by the Tory governments of this decade, resulting in the following:

(*a*) a reduced emphasis on regional planning and co-ordination;

(*b*) a degree of movement from regional offices to the use of *ad hoc* authorities;

(*c*) a change of emphasis from decision-taking in the regions to the exercise of more inspectorial functions.

There was a marked reduction in regionally-based staffs, notably in those departments which rely on regional offices, e.g. the Ministry of Labour, and in 1956 the Regional Organisation Committee of the Treasury, which was concerned with supervising the standard region programme, fell into disuse.

8. Increased devolution. The reaction against regional devolution was not absolute and in certain circumstances actually expanded. In particular, a Post Office Working Party in 1951 reported favourably on the use of devolved powers by regional directors and in 1957 the Ministry of Agriculture, Food and Fisheries was regionalised in order to overcome the inefficiency arising from the proliferation of a number of regionally-based, but unrelated, officers.

9. 1960s. The anti-regional trends of the 1950s were reversed, and emphasis was placed on economic and physical planning accompanied, for the first time, by a growth in regional "grass roots" political consciousness. The Labour Government in 1964 set up six Economic Planning Boards, with separate Boards for Wales and Scotland. The Boards were composed of members of the central departments concerned with planning responsibilities, and were assisted by Economic Planning Councils, constituted by representatives of industry, trade, local government, trade unions, etc.

10. Standardisation of decision-making powers. Less attention has been paid to the standardisation of the delegation of decision-taking powers than has been accorded to the problem of co-ordination of authorities through standardised areas. However, these matters are inseparable, and as has been pointed out "one of the advantages of a decentralised system is lost if one department insists on referring to headquarters problems that others settle locally, and this means that all must conform to the practice of the most cautious" (W. J. M. Mackenzie & J. W. Grove, *Central Administration in Britain*, Longmans, 1976).

REGIONALISM

11. The continuance of regionalism. Sharpe has identified two factors that justify the unlikelihood of further reactions against decentralisation.

(a) *Functional.* "The interposition of an agent of the central government responsible for the oversight of central government services for an area wider than individual local authorities is necessary if the planning and co-ordination functions are to take the burden from Whitehall, whilst being able to reflect back to the centre the particular interests and problems of the area" (*British Politics and Two Regionalisms*).

(b) *Political.* The need to satisfy demands for participation in the decision-making process which cannot be afforded by centralisation.

12. Regional and local government. The above discussion of decentralisation has concentrated on a downward extension of central functions to out-stations of the central government. However, the problem may be regarded also from the viewpoint of upward extension of local authorities as they come to exercise wider powers over larger regional areas.

13. Developments in the 1970s. The main developments in the 1970s have been the reform of the local government structure (*see* 23 and 25) and the proposals on devolution (*see* 30–33).

PROPOSALS FOR REFORM

14. Regionalism. This involves the devolution of decision-taking responsibilities to elected authorities covering wider areas than those covered by existing local authorities. The regions would be based on relatively homogeneous geographical areas. One of the most canvassed ideas is that of the "city region" (*see* **18**), i.e. regions based on important population centres.

15. Advantages of regionalism. These are as follows.

(*a*) Economic planning is more effective where larger regional authorities exist, having sufficient resources and powers to enable them to exert an influence on central policy.

(*b*) Regional authorities would constitute a more effective democratic counter-balance to the power of central government than is provided by the present local authorities.

(*c*) Environmental planning can only be effective over wider areas than those at present existing. Regional authorities would be able to achieve an overall rather than a piecemeal approach, and thus could justify the devolution of "real" powers.

(*d*) The economies of large-scale organisation could be reaped, both in the spheres of capital use and in elected and official manpower.

(*e*) The inadequacy of present local boundaries in regard to such matters as roads, further education, etc., could be overcome.

(*f*) Regional authorities would be in a stronger position to raise capital on the open market.

16. Arguments against regionalism. These are as follows.

(*a*) It is suggested that certain almost insoluble questions are basic to the whole concept of regionalism, namely:

(*i*) at what level should the authorities operate?

(*ii*) what should be their relations with the central government in order to achieve an adequate balance of power?

(*iii*) how should they be organised to achieve their objectives?

NOTE: Although difficult, these problems are capable at least of compromise solutions and are not inimical to a practical concept of regionalism.

(*b*) Certain functions go beyond regional boundaries, e.g. location of industry, investment programmes and priorities, and would thus operate to reduce regional authorities to a mere advisory status in many important fields.

(*c*) It is constantly argued that regional authorities would be too remote from the electorate to be effective democratic organisations. However, against this should be noted the following points:

(*i*) the increase in spatial mobility has expanded the concept of the locality;

(*ii*) there is no necessary connection between size and democracy;

(*iii*) provisions for second-tier authorities within the regions are constantly advanced by most proponents of regionalism.

(*d*) There is likely to be an internal lack of unity of purpose between representatives of areas within the regions which will detract from an overall objectivity in decision-making, e.g. in such matters as slum clearance priorities.

17. John P. Mackintosh, M.P. Mackintosh (*The Devolution of Powers*, Penguin and Chatto & Windus, 1968) favours extensive decentralisation of central powers which would effectively give all powers of "intermediate government" (including economic planning) to the regions. He conceives of the region being run in central government style with a Cabinet, ministers, etc., and not on the traditional committee system style, because "large structures cannot be run by groups of elected members deciding both policy and administrative detail". His views are criticised for the following reasons.

(*a*) They are incompatible with national economic planning and provide opposition rather than co-operation with a central plan.

(*b*) They will consequently exacerbate tensions between central and local government.

(*c*) Regional planning from a local government aspect differs fundamentally from national regional planning. The latter involves necessary differentiation between areas and the creation of a framework within which local government can contribute to overall policy.

NOTE: Mackintosh develops his theory on the view that the

national plan should not be imposed but should emerge as a result of the effects of wide decentralisation.

18. Derek Senior. In his dissenting view to the *Redcliffe-Maud Report*, Derek Senior recommended the creation of thirty-five regional authorities and one hundred and forty-eight second-tier authorities. He based his view on a belief that reorganisation should be based on social geography considerations; i.e. where people live and work, and what areas they function in. Senior classified each city region into *mature* (e.g. Leeds, London, Birmingham), *emergent* (e.g. Hull, Norwich, Middlesbrough), *embryonic* (e.g. Leicester, Coventry, Exeter) or *potential* (e.g. Ipswich, Plymouth, Ashford), each with a minimum population of 250,000.

He considered that these would represent generally appropriate catchment areas, suitable caseloads and adequate resources to be responsible for unified services such as urban renewal, promotion of regional development, etc.

19. Criticisms of the Senior approach. The following criticisms should be noted.

(*a*) *By Mackintosh.* Mackintosh based his criticism on his underlying view that an area should create, whereas city regions would merely be areas for the implementation of policy.

(*b*) *By the Redcliffe-Maud Commission.* In addition to considering Senior's proposals difficult to apply on an overall basis, the *Maud Report* considered:

(*i*) they could result in artificially contrived areas;

(*ii*) undesirable splitting into second-tier functional authorities was involved (*Maud* had of course based its emphasis on unitary authorities under eight large regions).

20. Distinction between city region and regional approaches. Although really the city region is one aspect of regionalism, it is useful conceptually to separate these. The distinction was made by Self, who considered that "the main alternatives lie between basing the new regions on major centres or adopting broader units, having some general recourse to the standard departmental regions . . . in general the first approach would coincide best with the facts of human geography, the needs of effective planning and the desirability of manageable and intelligible democratic units"

("Regional Planning and the Machinery of Government", *Public Administration*, Vol. 42, Autumn 1964, pp. 232–3).

21. Redcliffe-Maud Report. The *Report* proposed a three-part structure for local government, with unitary authorities carrying out all the major local government functions within the framework of eight provincial authorities. The provincial authorities would be responsible for drawing up the regional plan in co-operation with the government and for planning, research and co-ordination. The unitary authorities would perform the whole range of local government services, with the exception of the conurbations of Merseyside, Birmingham and South-East Lancashire and North-East Cheshire (SELNEC) which would, because of their large populations, be split into metropolitan authorities and metropolitan district authorities.

At local level, represented by the existing urban authorities, there would exist a largely functionless collection of authorities which would be representative of local opinion and would be entitled to consultation.

NOTE: The government White Paper issued subsequent to the *Report* did not accept the provincial structure and also added an additional two-part metropolitan authority for the South Hampshire complex based on Southampton and Portsmouth.

22. Advantages claimed in the Report. These are as follows:

(*a*) unification of planning and transport functions;

(*b*) enlarging of size of education authorities;

(*c*) the provision of a complete family service, linked to related services, e.g. education, health, etc.;

(*d*) the encouragement of housing development by the concentration of building and management functions in a much smaller number of stronger authorities;

(*e*) the better utilisation of manpower;

(*f*) the resulting shift of power, giving a better and more meaningful dialogue with the central government;

(*g*) the working out of a more liberal approach to sources of local finance.

23. The White Paper, 1971. In the light of the often irrational furore of existing local authorities and the belief of the government that local political support must be nurtured through local authorities, the Conservative Government rejected the proposals of the *Maud Report* and set out their own reform proposals in a White Paper—*Local Government in England: Proposals for Reorganisation* (Cmnd. 4584, 1971). The government proposed that forty-four new county councils, incorporating the existing independent county boroughs should be set up. They would have responsibility for education, personal social services, highways, traffic and transport, major planning functions and reserve powers in relation to housing, e.g. overspill policy. Within the counties rationalisation will be carried out of the existing local authorities through a programme of mergers, with the new "local" authorities being responsible for housing, development control and acquisition of land for planning purposes.

NOTE: An exception is made for the six predominantly metropolitan areas of Merseyside, SELNEC, West Midlands, West Yorkshire, South Yorkshire and the Tyneside/Wearside area. In such areas there will be a division between the county and local authorities, with the local authorities obtaining greater powers (e.g. education, personal social services) than throughout the rest of the country. London is not affected by the proposals.

24. Comments on the White Paper. The following points should be noted.

(*a*) *Wrong emphasis.* As is common, it treats the problem of local government reform as a separate issue from that of devolution of central powers, and consequently fails to deal with this problem.

(*b*) *Political motivation.* The White Paper gives the superficial impression of having been drawn up to appease local political opinion rather than to deal with the basic problems of local government.

(*c*) *Ambiguity.* It must be questioned whether in fact a real divergence from the Maud proposals has been suggested, as the counties exceed the size of the unitary authorities and the districts have comparatively little authority.

(*d*) *Remoteness.* The criticisms of remoteness have hardly been met.

25. Local Government Act 1972. The Act established the present structure of local government in England and Wales which now consists of the conurbations of six metropolitan counties and thirty-six metropolitan districts, and outside the conurbations of thirty-nine counties and two hundred and ninety-six districts, plus largely powerless parish and community councils. In *Wales* the new structure consists of eight counties and thirty-seven districts. In London the structure is headed by the Greater London Council, and supported by thirty-two London boroughs.

Although not as glaring as the disparities that existed prior to 1st April 1974 there still exists significant differences in the size of authorities, e.g. metropolitan counties range in population size from 1.2 million (Tyne and Wear) to 2.79 million (West Midlands); non-metropolitan counties range from 0.109 million (Isle of Wight) to 1.39 million (Kent); and metropolitan districts from 0.17 million to 1.09 million in Birmingham.

26. Ad hoc authorities. Functional decentralisation is achieved in Britain through the agency of various statutory authorities created to carry out specialised functions. They have been described as a "headless fourth branch of government" by Dr. Harold Seidman (*Cabinet Government*, 1936). The principal example is the nationalised industries (*see* XIII).

27. Reasons for functional decentralisation. Sir W. Ivor Jennings considered that the reasons for the creation of *ad hoc* authorities were as follows:

(*a*) to provide certain services outside the framework of political responsibility, e.g. B.B.C. and I.B.A.;
(*b*) to assist producers market products without political influence, e.g. the various agricultural marketing boards;
(*c*) to regulate professions subject to "slight political supervision", e.g. the Law Society;
(*d*) to organise technical public services which require little political intervention, e.g. the Forestry Commission;
(*e*) to depoliticise certain quasi-legal functions, e.g. transport licensing.

28. Classification of ad hoc bodies in the 1960s. (Hanson, A. H. and Walles M., *Governing Britain*, Fontana, 1973), have classified the various *ad hoc* bodies brought into existence during the 1960s as follows:

(*a*) *commercial*, e.g. the British Steel Corporation;

   (*b*) *promotional/commercial*, e.g. Training Boards;
   (*c*) *regulatory*, e.g. Air Transport Licensing Board;
   (*d*) *social*, e.g. Supplementary Benefits Commission;
   (*e*) *mixed*, e.g. Land Commission (now defunct);
   (*f*) *advisory/regulatory*, e.g. Commission for Racial Equality.

29. Ministerial control and relations. The principal concern with regard to the role of *ad hoc* authorities is that of the relationship of the boards (particularly the public corporations) with ministers, etc. This matter is fully developed in XIII.

DEVOLUTION

30. Introduction. An interesting variation of the traditional approaches to regionalism of significance in 1978 is devolution for Scotland and Wales. It is possible that devolution may result from the referenda proposed by the current legislation; the main implications therefore bear an outline study.

31. The Kilbrandon Report. The Royal Commission on the Constitution, 1969–73 (Cmnd. 5460, 1973) considered that the main arguments in favour of devolving legislative powers to separate assemblies for Scotland and Wales were:

   (*a*) it would act as a counter to over-centralisation with its consequent strains and remoteness;
   (*b*) government had become remote from the ordinary citizen;
   (*c*) it would recognise national feeling;
   (*d*) it would overcome the problems of administration resulting from physical remoteness.
The main counter-arguments advanced were:
   (*e*) there is little scope for the adoption of distinctive policies consistent with membership of the E.E.C., and thus emphasis is placed on the need for political and economic unity;
   (*f*) there would be a danger of incompatible policies;
   (*g*) fragmentation of policies would in fact lead to administrative rigidities.

32. The White Paper, 1974. The White Paper "*Democracy and Devolution: Proposals for Scotland and Wales*" (Cmnd. 5732) dealt with the major alternative schemes. Broadly it was felt that these could be:

   (*a*) legislative devolution; or

(*b*) devolution to elected assemblies in Scotland, Wales and the regions of responsibility for adjusting U.K. Parliamentary policies in the particular areas.

33. The Government's approach. The Government's proposals were published in *Our Changing Democracy: Devolution to Scotland and Wales* (Cmnd. 6348, 1975) and adopted in the legislation of 1977–8. The basic policy is the devolution of legislative powers to elected assemblies. The Scottish Assembly will be able to legislate to develop new, to modify, or to abolish existing, functions within the fields of authority devolved. In Wales the Assembly will be able to act within a framework established by Act of Parliament.

The fields of authority proposed to be delegated include functions within local government; health; personal social services; education; housing; physical planning and the environment; roads and transport; and industrial development.

NOTE: (1) Financial powers would not be delegated as public expenditure policies would be regulated by the U.K. Parliament subject to the assemblies receiving a block grant. (2) It was not intended that the Assemblies would take over the role of the local authorities. The Secretary of State for Wales commented in the third reading of the Bill that "in the devolved matters local government would relate to the assembly in the same way that local government now related to central government and there would be no problem of the duplication of functions".

PROGRESS TEST 11

1. Define and distinguish the terms "decentralisation", "deconcentration" and "regionalism". **(1)**
2. Why is decentralisation necessary? **(2)**
3. What basic problems must be overcome in establishing regional machinery? **(3)**
4. What factors basically justify the continuance of regionalism? **(11)**
5. Define "regionalism". Compare the arguments for and against regionalism. **(14–16)**
6. Consider the views on regionalism of J. P. Mackintosh. **(17)**
7. Consider the views on regionalism of D. Senior. **(18, 19)**

8. What is the basic difference between the regional and city-regional approaches? **(20)**

9. What proposals were made in the Redcliffe-Maud Report? What advantages did the report claim for its proposals? **(21, 22)**

10. Outline and comment on the proposals in the White Paper on Local Government Reform of 1971. **(23, 24)**

11. What is meant by functional decentralisation? What are the reasons for it? **(26–28)**

CHAPTER XII

The Relationship of Central and Local Government

INTRODUCTION

1. Basic features of the relationship. These are as follows.

(a) Absence of unified control. Although certain ministries exercise greater influence or control over local government than others, there is no single ministry charged with the overall review of local government activities. Similarly, where control exists it often stems from statutory powers rather than from the dominant status of the central authority (but *see* **17–18**).

(b) Two-way relationship. Over-emphasis of the "control" functions of central government hides the true nature of the relationship, which effectively rests upon a mutual flow of policy-making and technical information.

(c) Service provision. Local authorities essentially provide services in their own right and are responsible for the day-to-day administration and application of such services to the particular circumstances of their localities. Only in exceptional cases are they direct agents of the central government.

(d) Finance. A measure of financial independence is obtained by local authorities through their rating power. However, inflation and the pressure of achieving minimum standards coupled with the inherent defects of the rating system has led to a marked dependence on central grant assistance and loan sanction.

(e) Political relationships. A certain degree of bitterness and consequent over-emphasis of the negative aspects of the relationship may result from different political attitudes prevailing at the centre and in the local areas; e.g. the problem of acceptance of the comprehensive education programme during the Labour administration of 1964–70.

(f) National minima. A principle of central control is the need to achieve national minima in the provision of services and to ensure that local authorities are not permitted to fall below this level.

2. The effects of economic planning. Local authorities are in principle required to conform to the broad economic and social patterns established by the central government. Consequently, elements in the relationship which might have a liberalising effect are suppressed by the exigencies of national planning. Features of such planning over the last twenty years have included the following:

(a) the adoption of patterns of economic development;

(b) the projection of economic trends and the requirement that short-term policy should fall within the boundaries of such projections;

(c) the establishment as a result of the *Plowden Report* of 1961 of long-term surveys of public expenditure and probable resources, and the need to make long-term decisions in the light of such surveys.

3. The inflexibility of planning. The effect of systematic national expenditure planning is emphasis on its relative inflexibility, and consequently to render local authority expenditure and programmes subordinate to this overall structure. Planning is inflexible in the following ways:

(a) priorities determinable at any particular point in time are marginal and do not permit of excessive policy changes;

(b) major policy decisions involve long-term sunk costs;

(c) any expenditure decision must be taken in the context of limited public financial resources.

4. The financial aspect of the relationship. Since 1945 grants to local authorities have increased at a faster rate than local expenditure, and now constitute approximately 60 per cent of combined grant and rate income. In addition since 1974 the Labour Government has used the Rate Support Grant machinery for enforcing economies in local authority spending.

THE CENTRAL DEPARTMENTS INVOLVED

5. The departments. The principal departments involved with local authorities are the Department of the Environment, incorporating the very important local government ministries of Housing and Local Government, the Ministry of Transport, and the Department of Education and Science. Relationships with local authorities vary between the departments, and this consideration will probably continue to apply despite merging of departments.

6. Housing and local government. Traditionally, the ministry left the local authorities considerable initiative in public health, housing and planning. It did not operate an inspectorial system and constantly rejected a supervisory role. It exercised informal influence in the field of local organisation, but elsewhere was principally concerned with the approval of schemes (*see* **19**(*b*)) and in the application of legislation to local authorities. Recently, however, in the light of social and economic policy, the role of the ministry as adviser and provider of tools has changed towards interventionism through the use of such forces as loan sanction.

7. Transport. The relationship is affected and modified by the fact that both central and local authorities are providers of services in their own rights. In fact, even in the ministry field of major roads, a considerable impetus has sprung from local authorities. However, cost control through the grant system has proved important, as has the increasing role of highways in national planning.

8. Social services. In a historical context the role of the Home Office with regard to social services, subsequently transferred to the Department of Health and Social Security, provides an interesting example of the development of control, although this control is at the present day much less significant due to the strengthening of local administration by the concentration of social services at county levels as a result of the Local Authorities Social Services Act. The control developed as a result of the concentration originally of skilled manpower at the centre, and led the Home Office to see its role in relation to local authorities as that of maintaining material standards; disseminating information and advice; and supervising services in the general context of government policy.

9. The Department of Education and Science. Section 1 of the Education Act 1944, *prima facie* gives the Department of Education and Science powerful control powers, and other powers of considerable importance are detailed in specific sections of the Act; e.g. the prescribing of standards for school premises, the role of the inspectorate and indication of education plans by the local authority in a Development Plan.

The importance of the Department of Education and Science in the relationship is increased by the political nature of education policy and its high cost as a proportion of local authority services. However, the trend has been to a large extent to concentrate on informal powers through the issue of circulars, and to leave the local authorities considerable independence within proscribed boundaries.

CONCEPTS OF CONTROL

10. Laissez-faire approach. This attitude is typified by the old Ministry of Health, which adopted a comparatively less interventionist attitude in relation to such matters as collection, analysis and dissemination of information, research and insistence on compliance with departmental policies. It is possible that this attitude was a result of the small proportion of grant-aided welfare expenditure. This view, however, probably places too great a correlation on finance and control, and tends to mask the ultimate arbiter, which is national interest in the level and nature of services provided.

NOTE: Unfortunately the *laissez-faire* approach is often justified on the fallacious ground that local authorities will only progress if left to learn by their own mistakes, and the reliance on the electorate as the final judge of local authority standards.

11. Hybrid approach. The approach of the old Ministry of Housing and Local Government was *laissez-faire* to the extent that it permitted local authorities to determine their broad needs and how these are to be met. In the field of housing provision, however, a hybrid or intermixed approach was noticeable in that central officials would not question local housing decisions unless they appeared to be clearly beyond the capacities of the local authorities and local building industries; it was regulatory in the control of standards, lay-out and design, and it was promotional in the large extent of advisory material issued and in the sponsoring of consortia and industrialised building.

12. Regulatory approach. The Home Office typified this approach in respect of the children's services which are now under the control of the D.H.S.S. Emphasis was placed on the inspectorate for the following reasons:

(*a*) the service was comparatively new and standards uncertain;

(*b*) local authority departments were too weak to admit of great independence;

(*c*) central help was necessary in order to promote minimum standards.

13. Concepts of central control. The relationship of central government and local authorities may be conceptualised as follows.

(*a*) *Constitutional.* Its existence is between two groups of government institutions, each having separate legal existence.

(*b*) *Political.* The powers of one group complement and conflict with the powers of the other. Basically this dichotomy must be resolved in the democratic context by co-operation rather than coercion. However, the departments are in a stronger position and make far more of the important decisions.

NOTE: Any consideration of the reform of the relationship is unreal to the extent that it fails to accept that the government will reject any reform which makes more difficult the execution of government policies.

(*c*) *Administrative.* The relationship concerns the actual execution of policies. However, the assumption that local authorities are merely agents for the execution of policy decided by government departments is incorrect in that it ignores both that local authorities make and influence the making of policy, and that departments themselves are deeply involved in the administrative process at the local level.

14. The necessary functions of central government. The government has the following responsibilities.

(*a*) *Promotion of the national interest.* The government is basically responsible for defining and promoting the national interest, for ensuring that local and factional interests do not impede the promotion of the general interest. This recognition of national importance necessarily subordinates local authorities politically to the central government, although legally they retain independence.

(*b*) *Fixing of standards.* Professor Griffiths (in *Central Departments and Local Authorities*, Allen & Unwin, 1966) considered that the basic reason that central departments retain control over local authorities is that they cannot trust all local authorities not to economise to such an extent that the quality of services would be inadequate; e.g. it is the universal practice of all government departments to insist on minimum constructional standards. This control over the adequacy of services provided is at the heart of the whole relationship. Adequacy itself involves two separate factors namely:

(*i*) services are inadequate if less than the requirements of national policy;

(*ii*) they are unacceptable if provision exceeds the allotted share of resources, or if they seek to achieve ends other than those laid down as national policy.

NOTE: Where a service complies with national standards but varies in adequacy the right of intervention arises and provides a basic dilemma between local democracy and efficiency. Although perhaps an overriding principle of control it would seem that in view of the economies imposed by central government in recent years it may be suggested that in times of financial stringency the criteria becomes that of preventing overspending.

15. The position of local authorities. Factors influencing the relationship of individual local authorities with the central government include the following.

(*a*) *Size*. Size differences create differences in relationships with the central government. Large authorities (500,000 plus) are able to employ larger staffs, operate larger programmes and are so well known in the departments that their wishes carry great weight. In particular, their chief officers, committee chairmen, etc., have national political importance. These authorities, being in a better position to persuade and influence, are consequently allowed greater freedom and flexibility of action than the smaller, weaker authorities, which are sometimes adversely treated because of their comparative inexperience and paucity of resources.

(*b*) *Party political influence*. The degree of coincidence and influence with the central political organisation.

(*c*) *Physical closeness to London*. This is more effective in maintaining the two-way relationship with the central government.

NOTE: Attitudes may have developed over a period of time, independent of any of the above grounds. In addition, external pressure is more noticeable in popular functions, such as education and traffic, rather than in the more altruistic functions such as mental health.

16. Role of the local authority associations. These are important as collective voices of local authorities in influencing legislation, government policies and administration, and as channels of local authority opinion. Their activities fall into the following three main categories.

(*a*) *In relation to central departments.* Government departments operate in close connection with the associations, with frequent consultations. However, the associations complain that on occasions they are not consulted in advance on technical publications containing policy statements. In general, however, secretaries of the associations are consulted about changes in government policy affecting local authorities, whether involving legislative or administrative introduction.

(*b*) *In relation to Parliament.* They operate here to seek amendment of bills affecting local authorities and the sponsoring and promotion of measures affecting local authorities. In this respect they employ parliamentary vice-presidents.

(*c*) *In relation to members.* In this respect they are principally concerned with advice on legal matters and on administrative and policy questions.

METHODS OF CONTROL

17. Informal central control. Methods of control exist outside the statutory field and are exercised through various conventional forms. Such control is exercised in the following three main ways.

(*a*) Circulars are issued, consisting of letters drawing attention to suggested desirable procedures. They take the form also of practice codes, memoranda, etc., designed both to raise efficiency standards and to explain or reinforce ministerial policy.

(*b*) Departments and ministries act as "clearing houses" for the dissemination of information, and for guidance of local authorities in respect of administrative problems.

(*c*) Informal advice is given to local authorities through the inspectorial system.

18. Why informal control is effective. Although not based on any statutory foundation, informal influence upon local authorities tends to achieve directive status. The acceptance of this non-mandatory control by local authorities rests upon the following factors.

(a) *Partnership*. The functional overlapping between central and local government creates a relationship dependent on the development of a partnership approach to various rights and duties.

(b) *Informal consultations*. The practice of consultations prior to the introduction of legislation tightens the relationship between central and local authorities and enables the setting of standards which may be clarified by ministerial advice.

(c) *Sharing of knowledge*. Administrative and technical knowledge acquired by central departments is made available to local authorities.

(d) *Conformity*. The background of central control is the necessity of ensuring conformity with centrally established standards, particularly where the central authority is able to back up such conformity with financial sanctions. Thus in order to secure vital financial aid, local authorities must conform with ministerial policy, expressed in informal means of control.

(e) *Ultimate sanction*. In the final analysis, conformity with informal control is reinforced by the possibility of the central authority seeking recourse to additional or existing statutory powers.

19. Statutory powers. Central departments generally seek to rely on specific powers when exercising formal control, rather than on the general powers expressed in certain statutes, e.g. the Education Act 1944. For the purpose of this section it is proposed to deal only with the principal forms of statutory control, namely, financial control and control through the approval of schemes.

(a) *Financial control*. This is exercised through the following.

(i) Control through grants, which was achieved historically through the medium of specific grants, has now been altered in emphasis, as the greater part of grant aid to local authorities is given through the Rate Support Grant which is of course a general grant. However both the global amount of the grant and its method of allocation are controlled by the central government and the grant is thus a broad-edged tool for influencing local authority expenditure decisions. Its importance has been particularly illustrated over recent years when by a culmination of exhortation and grant control the expenditure of local authorities has been prescribed by the overall national economic strategy and has involved limited growth programmes and capital investment by local authorities.

(*ii*) Loan sanction is effected under the provisions of the Local Government Act 1972, which requires ministerial sanction before loan-raising powers are used. As local authorities are forced to borrow for all major projects, a potent form of control is placed in the hands of the minister, such control being enhanced in times of national stringency.

NOTE: A limited measure of freedom in respect of loans was implemented during 1971, but is not sufficient to invalidate the general premise of loans as a potent form of control.

(*b*) *Approval of schemes.* This technique requires local authorities to submit schemes for carrying out particular services to the appropriate central government department. This system is justified on the grounds of taking account of local variations, the devolution of administrative responsibilities and the exercise of local initiative. In practice, however, it necessitates conformity with central policy and standards before a scheme is accepted. Important examples exist under the Education Act 1944, in regard to local educational needs, and under the Town and Country Planning Act 1971, in regard to Development Plans.

20. Other statutory powers. These include matters which, though not being individually important, contribute to the cumulative effect of control. They include inspection, control over officers (very limited), issue of regulations, issue of directions, confirmation of by-laws, hearing of appeals and the rarely used default powers.

CONCLUSIONS

21. Cumulative effect of controls. Central control falls short of dictatorship over local authorities, but the various powers do have a marked cumulative effect. The result of such cumulative effect is that, whilst local authorities exercise a degree of autonomy, they are in general forced to comply with overall central policy. As a result, also, local authorities tend to look to the centre for guidance even when this is not legally or practically required. This attitude of dependence and the wide powers of central influence tend to make local authorities act as local administrative bodies responsible for considering local variations, but basically agents of central policy.

22. Justification of central control. The following points should be noted.

(a) *Role of the state.* The increase in state functions, which now range from social welfare to the promotion of economic prosperity, have a notable centralising tendency and can only be effectively operated from the centre.

(b) *Defects of local authorities.* The incapability of local authorities, through structural inadequacy and resource disparities, to maintain common standards.

(c) *Financial assistance.* Increasing financial dependence of local authorities on central grants, and the inelasticity and inadequacy of the rating system.

(d) *Uniformity.* The need to achieve common standards can only be achieved through government direction.

(e) *Greater resources.* The larger resources of the central government both financially and on the technical and administrative sides.

(f) *National interest.* The requirement that sectional interests be subordinated to those of the nation as a whole and the necessity of central control for the implementation of such domination.

23. Disadvantages of central control. In modern social and economic conditions a measure of central control is probably both inevitable and desirable. Disadvantages stem, however, from excessive control, in particular the following:

(a) local variations are often ignored as a result of the remoteness and size of the central machine;

(b) local initiative may be destroyed;

(c) loss of interest may be attributed to a lack of local power, and the accompanying feelings of impotence and lack of importance.

24. The outlook and suggested principles. The following points have been made.

(a) The Local Government Manpower Committee, 1948, suggested that the relationship should be one where "local authorities are responsible bodies competent to discharge their own functions . . . they exercise their responsibilities in their own right . . . the objective (of central control) should be to leave as much as possible of the detailed management of a scheme or service to the local authority and to concentrate the department's control at key points where it can most effectively discharge its responsibilities for government policy and financial administration".

(b) The Maud Committee on Management considered that there was a need to check the steady reduction of discretion allowed to local authorities and to prevent their conversion into mere agencies of the central government. In particular, the Committee thought that though Whitehall should in the national interest control local investment policy it ought not to extend this control to details of local building and expenditure. In consequence it recommended a strengthening of local taxing powers and a greater realism in respect of loan sanction.

(c) The Redcliffe-Maud Commission considered that implementation of its proposals would result in a shift of power and responsibility from the central government to the strengthened local councils, and would involve a more meaningful dialogue between the two. Lord Redcliffe-Maud himself subsequently asserted that the central government would be happy to transfer such authority. The Commission considered that the key factor in lack of local autonomy was the size and ability of local units to meet their enhanced responsibilities.

25. The dynamics of the relationship. Although attention has been drawn to the formal and informal methods of control it is important to consider the nature of the central–local relationship as a dynamic process. In this respect the following basic assumptions may be suggested.

(a) Each local authority and each central department is an individual decision-making unit with its own values.

(b) Each individual authority has different strategies open to it in the pursuit of these values.

(c) The two-way process may be viewed as one of *control* flowing from the centre which is reciprocated by *influence* flowing inwards from the localities.

(*d*) The overall pattern is in turn largely structured by the financial system in which the system operates.

A pattern may thus be built up describing in general terms the relationship. Bearing in mind that the centre is internally differentiated and that this produces a fragmentation of central–local relationships, the central influence may be seen as a two part process, viz. conflicts leading to the use of regulations, schemes, etc., resolving into the local authority decision (*control function*) and on the other hand the objective of influencing local values and dispositions through the use of grants and informal methods of control and resulting in the ultimate local authority decision (*influence function*).

For its own part the local authorities exercise influence through local political parties, M.P.s, petitions, deputations, and act collectively as pressure groups (*counterbalancing function*).

26. The future. It is suggested that the most important factor in the future of local government is that of enabling the system to adapt sufficiently to undertake all it should and could perform. Since 1945 there have been appreciable changes in the factors affecting the role of local government, each tending to reinforce central concentration, as follows:

(*a*) the development and acceptance of the ideal of national physical, financial and economic planning;

(*b*) the demand for more and better public services and the political response to such demand (particularly with regard to schools, roads and urban renewal);

(*c*) the demographic and other movements which have made regional movements more apparent and which have resulted in increased political activity.

All these must be borne in mind in considering extensions of local autonomy.

PROGRESS TEST 12

1. What basic features may be discerned in central and local government relations?   (**1**)

2. How does economic planning affect the relationship?   (**2, 3**)

3. What central departments are mainly concerned with local government?   (**5–9**)

4. What different approaches and concepts of control exist? **(10–13)**

5. What are the necessary functions of central government? **(14)**

6. What factors influence the position of local authorities? **(15)**

7. What is the role of the local authority associations? **(16)**

8. What are the principle methods of informal control? Why is such control effective? **(17, 18)**

9. What are the principal forms of statutory control? **(19, 20)**

10. What are the justifications of central control? **(22)**

11. What are the disadvantages of central control? **(23)**

12. What principles of central control have been suggested? **(24)**

CHAPTER XIII

Public Corporations

INTRODUCTION

This chapter does not attempt an exhaustive study of public corporations, but concentrates on the economic and political significance of the public sector, and on the problems of responsibility and control.

1. Characteristics of public corporations. Professor A. H. Hanson (*Nationalisation*, Allen & Unwin, 1963) identified public corporations as having six principal characteristics.

(*a*) They are wholly state-owned.

(*b*) They are not subject to parliamentary financial scrutiny such as that to which departments are submitted.

(*c*) They are statutorily created and outside the ambit of ordinary company law.

(*d*) They have corporate status and thus can be sued, hold property, enter into contracts, etc.

(*e*) In theory at least they are independently financed through their revenue and through capital borrowing.

(*f*) Employees of public corporations are not civil servants but are employed directly by, and subject to conditions of, the corporations.

2. Their significance in public administration. This results from the following:

(*a*) the nature of the relationships between the corporations, ministers and Parliament;

(*b*) the role of the public corporations in the general sphere of government economic control;

(*c*) the organisational structure of corporations in so far as it represents management organisations and problems in the public sector;

(*d*) their basic nature as instruments of government, i.e. their status as social, economic, or hybrid organisations.

PUBLIC OWNERSHIP

3. Arguments in favour of public ownership. These can be stated as follows.

(a) *Political:*

(i) the achievement of basic socialist ideals as to the more equitable distribution of wealth, and the eradication of unearned private income;

(ii) production for use rather than for profit.

(b) *Social:*

(i) public interest in the ownership of key industries;

(ii) the social desirability of supporting certain industries which could otherwise only run at a loss.

(c) *Pragmatic:*

(i) the reaping of the advantages of large-scale production, especially where large capital investment is required, or large areas covered;

(ii) securing of public revenue;

(iii) means of securing and influencing national policy.

NOTE: In practice public ownership has arisen for practical rather than ideological reasons; e.g. nationalisation during the period 1945–51 was largely pragmatic, particular examples being the nationalisation of the railways to achieve transport reconstruction and integration and the elimination of cartels and restrictive practices in the steel industry. The steel industry is of particular interest in that its subsequent denationalisation by the Tory Government of 1951 and renationalisation by the Labour Government in 1967 appears to owe as much to political as to pragmatic considerations.

4. Arguments against public ownership. These can be stated as follows.

(a) The advantages of the free working of economic forces are lost.

(b) Public bodies do not provide suitable means of running public concerns.

(c) It is difficult to establish suitable working relationships, e.g. between the industries and Parliament.

NOTE: The above arguments (a) and (b) only apply where the

whole of an industry is nationalised and cannot justify piecemeal public control.

5. Forms of public ownership. The following can be distinguished.

(*a*) *Departmental method.* In this case a minister is directly responsible for all aspects of policy and administration, employees are civil servants and the Treasury has direct financial control; i.e. the acquired industry is on the same status as any other government department. The Post Office was the principal example of this form of organisation until it became a public corporation.

(*b*) *Public corporation method.* The industry is run by an administrative board with a minister responsible for overall policy, but not for day-to-day administration. The board has a self-contained financial structure. This method is based on the desirability of combining commercial freedom with public accountability, the underlying assumption being that such freedom is inhibited by an excessive degree of centralised ministerial control.

NOTE: Ownership may also be effected by government purchase of shares in private firms, enabling it to participate in profits and to influence policy without the necessity of assuming sole and direct responsibility, e.g. British Petroleum.

CONTROL AND SUPERVISION OF PUBLIC CORPORATIONS

6. Administrative structure. In general, the corporations are governed by boards of ten to twelve people. Problems have arisen with regard to the attraction of suitable memberships due to such matters as image, salaries, etc. This has in turn resulted in key significance being placed on a board's chairman. The commercial freedom or otherwise of a corporation may thus largely turn on the formal and informal relations worked out between a minister and individual chairmen.

7. Centralised structures. An early feature of the post-1945 corporations was an emphasis on centralised government control and administrative structure. This was considered desirable for the following reasons:

(*a*) to facilitate large-scale planning;

(*b*) to achieve co-ordination and co-operation between the industries;

(*c*) to involve the industries effectively in the national economic development;

(*d*) to ensure public accountability.

NOTE: This approach was criticised as leading to remote and bureaucratic control, excessive middle management and duplication of functions between the boards and associated departments.

8. Recent trends. The present tendency is away from centralised structures towards administrative decentralisation. In 1955 railway organisation was decentralised by the introduction of six area boards. However, despite similar trends in electricity, gas, dock administration, etc., such decentralisation was not universal and in particular the Fleck Committee in 1955 considered the National Coal Board to be too decentralised and consequent control over local areas was enhanced. Other recent trends of importance include the following.

(*a*) The establishment of a National Freight Corporation under the 1968 Transport Act aimed at ensuring the integration of road and railway freight operations. The railways board is now concerned with the actual operation of the trains alone.

(*b*) Under the 1968 Act the National Bus Company was established, aimed at achieving a much greater degree of centralisation and co-ordination.

(*c*) The Water Act 1973 created new authorities to take over the functions relating to water conservation, water supply, sewerage and sewage disposal. Responsibility is now vested in nine regional water authorities. Although not technically government agencies their creation represents a further centralist move.

(*d*) In 1973 the British Gas Corporation replaced the existing Gas Council and boards.

9. Parliamentary supervision. Parliamentary supervision is effectively constrained by such matters as time, the technical nature of the issues involved, and the failure to determine the proper areas of control. The following bodies are involved.

(*a*) *The finance committees.* The old Select Committee on Estimates, the Public Accounts Committee and the Comptroller and Auditor General do not carry out examinations of the estimates or account of the public corporations, though the Public Accounts Committee retains the power to look at accounts and reports in general terms.

> NOTE: However, in so far as the industries rely on the Treasury for capital, Parliament and the Comptroller and Auditor General do have direct involvement with the financial affairs of the corporations.

(b) *Committee on Nationalised Industries.* The Committee represents the most effective medium of parliamentary supervision. Its role of working in close co-operation with the boards, the Treasury and the relevant departments has led to increased parliamentary and public knowledge of the corporations.

10. Some proposals for reform. Proposals to increase parliamentary supervision and ministerial control have included the following:

(a) the attachment of Comptroller and Auditor General functions to the Select Committee;

(b) the creation of ministers as board chairmen;

(c) the creation of a Ministry for Nationalised Industries (*see* 29);

(d) the appointment of a specialised committee (as in France) to examine the efficiency of the industries;

(e) the securing of greater consideration of annual capital expenditure programmes of the industries by the introduction of a Nationalised Industries Investment Bill, or by the creation of a National Advisory Council for Capital Spending.

The only proposal currently in operation is that for the specialised committee represented by the Nationalised Industries Committee, though no move has been made to attach specialised committees to individual industries.

11. Ministerial responsibility. The main problem is the reconciliation of ministerial responsibility and its attendant control with that of managerial autonomy. The two basic principles of ministerial responsibility are as follows:

(a) securing the public interest;

(b) overseeing the efficiency of the industry.

The minister's powers can be divided as follows.

(a) *Statutory powers.* These are probably in many cases of less significance than informal extra-statutory powers, though they of course form the basis of these. The principal statutory powers are concerned with the appointment of boards, giving directions in the national interest, approval of investment programmes, control of borrowing, education and training policy, approval of form of accounts and control of research and development.

(b) *Extra-statutory powers.* The minister has important informal powers and influence, operating in such basic fields as broad policy, pricing, etc. The Select Committee on Nationalised Industries considered that a feature of the constituting legislation was that "vital administrative questions, such as the relationship between the managing boards and ministers and Parliament, remains subject for disagreement and negotiation". This results in ministers and industries arriving at informal arrangements concerning such matters as balance of powers, duties of the industries and the nature of ministerial control.

12. Interpretations of control. As a broad division, ministerial control has been concerned with financial and economic matters. Views on the proper extent of ministerial control have ranged as follows.

(a) *The commercial view.* The board's autonomy is emphasised.
(b) *The middle view.* Balancing of commercial motives and the public interest.
(c) *The departmental view.* Boards treated in practice as ministerial departments, with full and detailed control.

13. Three basic questions. These three diverging views point to three basic questions of control which have to be resolved, namely:

(a) to what extent should the boards be commercial bodies?
(b) to what extent should ministers be concerned with policy, public interest and operational efficiency questions?
(c) should control be intimate or exercised at arm's length?

THE SELECT COMMITTEE'S VIEWS

14. Introduction. In 1968 the Committee interpreted the recent trends in the relationship as a growth in rationally determined strategic guidance together with greater autonomy for the boards in interpreting and complying with this guidance as efficiently as possible and by means which they themselves choose.

The Committee considered that the twin basic responsibilities of the minister *vis-à-vis* the industries were the securing of the public interest and the securing of industrial efficiency. Allied were two subsidiary functions, namely acting as spokesman for the industries in Parliament and the Cabinet, and representing parliamentary and Cabinet views to the boards.

15. Criticisms of control. These can be stated as follows.

(*a*) Imprecise definition of extent has led to criticism in both the statutory field of investment control and the informal field of price control.

(*b*) Lack of clarity contributes to confusion of purposes, policies, methods and responsibilities; e.g. British Airways have consistently sought to obtain clear policy guidance on the allocation of overseas routes, particularly with the development of independent airlines such as British Caledonian.

(*c*) Confusion of responsibilities between board and minister tends to reflect in two resultant controversies, namely:

    (*i*) the responsibilities of the Treasury;

    (*ii*) the staffing of the sponsoring departments.

16. Conclusions of the Select Committee. These are as follows.

(*a*) *Advantages of control.*

    (*i*) The positive influence of the minister, particularly in the fields of economic thinking and methods.

    (*ii*) The importance of control with regard to resolution of conflict between social obligations and efficiency.

(*b*) *Disadvantages of control.*

    (*i*) The fact that the advantages would take too long to come to fruition.

    (*ii*) The existence of strained relationships.

    (*iii*) The danger of an increase in government involvement in detailed management.

    (*iv*) The ineffectiveness of ministerial control in policy and operations co-ordination.

    (*v*) The lack of clarity of purpose and responsibilities.

17. Principles of control. These are as follows.

(*a*) Control and management cannot be divorced.

(*b*) The overall efficiency of the industries has suffered from a lack of accepted principles.

(*c*) A feature of the statutory basis has been the absence of a definition of relationships.

(*d*) Responsiveness to public interest is really only obtainable through ministerial control.

(*e*) Conclusions as to Parliament's intentions may be drawn from the particular form of nationalisation used.

18. Strategic or tactical control. The former consists of laying down broad economic guidelines, including financial objectives, broad pricing and investment criteria, investment reviews, and overall policy requirements. This form of control is associated with the Department of Trade.

Tactical control involves the application of detailed duties and responsibilities in specific areas of management the use of detailed financial control, close investment scrutiny and the issue of specific directions. This form is associated with the Ministry of Transport. The Committee was broadly in favour of the trend to strategic control, though it felt that tactical control may be appropriate in the case of industries in deficit.

19. Parliamentary accountability. The Committee considered that all ministerial control should be seen against the background of responsibility to Parliament. Ministers are liable to account to Parliament for all the actual exercise of their control over the industries, and also for the possible or potential use of formal and the better established informal powers.

20. Conclusions on ministerial responsibility. "The aim should be to allow the boards of the industries to operate within a more certain framework of social and economic requirements, and then to leave them free to attain the best results they can within that framework. Their results should be subject to examination by various devices of accountability" (W. Thornhill, *The Nationalised Industries*, Nelson, 1968).

The Committee established the following ten principles.

(*a*) Ministers must be primarily concerned with the public interest.

(b) Economic efficiency should be the responsibility of the minister through broad oversight, but not through involvement in management.

(c) Within the above limits the industries should be left as free as possible.

(d) Clear demarcation of responsibilities should be established.

(e) Strategic control rather than tactical control should be applied.

(f) Control should not be wholly formal.

(g) Ministers and industries should be publicly accountable.

(h) The measure of management success should be the efficiency with which its joint social-economic functions are carried out.

(i) Improvement in management should be the objective of the minister.

(j) Fruitful control depends on the attitudes of boards and ministers.

ECONOMIC AND FINANCIAL FRAMEWORK OF PUBLIC CORPORATIONS

21. Basic features. These are as follows.

(a) The economic obligations of the industries are the main determinants of their activities.

(b) The constituting statutes are inadequate in regard to financial obligations.

(c) The choice of instruments for economic control has varied over the years.

22. Recommendations of the White Paper, 1961. The White Paper *Financial and Economic Obligations of the Nationalised Industries* (Cmnd. 1337) laid down the principle that "although the industries have obligations of a national and non-commercial kind, they are not . . . to be regarded as social services absolved from economic and social justification".

The industries had been criticised because of their inadequate reserves position, their heavy reliance on Treasury borrowings and their low returns. The White Paper in consequence recommended the following.

(a) The duty of the industries to pay their way should be applied over five-year periods.

(*b*) Provision should be made from revenue for capital development.

(*c*) Investment review procedures should be codified.

(*d*) Ministers should take an interest in pricing policies.

(*e*) Boards should be compensated in respect of unprofitable "social" activities carried out at the government's request.

23. Criticisms of the White Paper. The 1961 White Paper was criticised on the following grounds.

(*a*) The concepts of financial objectives were equivocal and could be interpreted either positively, as the achievement of profits, or negatively, as the mere preservation of capital.

(*b*) Whilst concentrating on end results it gave little guidance as to the means for achieving these ends.

(*c*) Financial objectives gave inadequate guidance as to investment policies.

24. Recommendations of the White Paper, 1967. The White Paper *A Review of Economic and Financial Objectives* stated the following.

(*a*) Emphasis should be placed on "laying down criteria which will have a regulatory effect" rather than the exercise of ministerial control by "end result" objectives. Financial objectives are only "economically justifiable to the extent that they reflect sound investment and pricing policies".

(*b*) Emphasis should be placed on optimising the allocation of resources and the need for developing the economic thinking of the industries.

(*c*) Emphasis should be placed on "strategic control" (*see* **18**).

SOCIAL OBLIGATIONS OF PUBLIC CORPORATIONS

25. Definition. The Select Committee made the following observations.

(*a*) Social obligations should not be equated with unremunerative operations.

(*b*) Social obligations cover goods, services and methods of production.

(*c*) Such obligations may involve not doing something profitable, as well as carrying out unprofitable tasks.

(*d*) Pricing may take into account social obligations.

(*e*) Social obligations may be imposed by statute.

26. Responsibility. In determining social obligations, two relevant questions are involved.

(*a*) Who should be responsible for determining the nature and extent of social obligations?

(*b*) Who should pay for social obligations?

The Committee took the view that ministers and boards should be commonly motivated, except where variations were necessary to promote social welfare. The minister should interpret public interest in meeting such obligations, and the boards should be compensated for carrying out such tasks.

27. Selection and definition. The minister should be responsible for precise definition of social obligations to be imposed upon the boards for the following reasons:

(*a*) he carries wider responsibility for the social, economic and public interest;

(*b*) value judgments are his province;

(*c*) relevant figures for wider costs come from outside the industries;

(*d*) there is a likelihood of bias in the industries;

(*e*) the minister is responsible for handling public funds.

THE RELATIONSHIP BETWEEN GOVERNMENT AND PUBLIC CORPORATIONS

28. The developing relationship. The relationship of ministers and industries has become in general one of strategic guidance coupled with commercial autonomy. This relationship is not always reflected in the institutional structure of control, and often leads to a confusion of purpose between ministries, the Treasury and the boards.

The dual responsibilities of the minister (*see* **14**) and their concentration in a single minister was considered by the Select Committee to be the principal cause of confusion.

29. A ministry for nationalised industries. The Committee considered that the new structure for control should be the creation of a single ministry responsible for the overseeing efficiency functions, with other functions remaining in the existing departments. The new ministry would deal with the following:

(a) appointment and dismissal of boards;

(b) pricing and investment policies, approval of capital structures and borrowing, reviewing investment programmes and agreeing financial objectives;

(c) furthering inter-industry co-ordination and co-operation;

(d) efficiency studies and general oversight of organisational efficiency;

(e) accounting to Parliament.

30. Advantages. These are as follows:

(a) optimum use of resources;

(b) increased specialisation and the development, through unity of experience and common purpose, of a more consistent relationship to the industries;

(c) effective co-ordination of commercial policies and promotion of common management and control techniques;

(d) inter-industry co-ordination of pricing policies, demand forecasts and investment programmes;

(e) the possibility that the minister could act as a spokesman for all the industries.

31. Treasury objections. These were as follows:

(a) such separation as envisaged by the Committee was impracticable;

(b) ministers should continue to be responsible for sectors whether in public or private ownership, but the Committee considered sector control to be a policy responsibility;

(c) it would withdraw from policy-making departments the experience and overall view of the industries that they must have in order to have full regard for the sector of the economy for which they are responsible.

32. Consequences for other departments. These would be as follows.

(a) Other related departments would continue to be responsible for the initiation of policy towards the nationalised industries in so far as they were required to do so in the public interest.

(b) The sponsoring departments would be responsible primarily for preparation, negotiation and formulation of sector policies; e.g. Transport would remain with the minister because of its wide outside ramifications.

33. The White Paper, 1969. The government expressed its views in the White Paper *Ministerial Control of the Nationalised Industries* (Cmnd. 4027). In particular the government did not accept the proposal for a Ministry of Nationalised Industries, its main thesis being that, although the responsibilities defined by the Committee could be conceptually separated, the disadvantages arising from the change in machinery outweighed the advantages, particularly as follows.

(*a*) Decisions previously involving one ministry would involve two.

(*b*) In practice, a distinction between sector and efficiency responsibilities would often be impossible, e.g. in power and transport.

(*c*) The position of chairmen of the boards would be made more difficult and equivocal through having to deal with two departments.

(*d*) Intervention in detailed management would not be reduced by the proposed change, and in fact might well be increased.

NOTE: The government did, however, concede that there might be advantages in establishing an organisation which would treat nationalised industries as a function of government in themselves.

34. Specific proposals accepted. The government did, however, welcome the following recommendations:

(*a*) that there should be discussions between the Treasury and the sponsoring departments with regard to control of investments;

(*b*) that the sponsoring departments should bring the industries together to discuss common problems, and that the industries should have opportunities to meet the economic departments;

(*c*) that the government would permit formal directions to be given in non-statutory defined areas, but as a whole would prefer ministerial relations to be worked out within the existing framework.

NOTE: With regard to the recommendations of the *White Paper* on economic and financial objectives, the government accepted the general approach to pricing policy, but not the recommendation that control over prices be given legislative sanction as this would involve both practical difficulties and undesirable interference in management.

35. White Paper: The Nationalised Industries (1978). The White Paper made two main sets of proposals:

(*a*) for improving the relations between the government and the nationalised industries;

(*b*) for reinforcing the commercial disciplines in the industries.

36. Relations with the industries. The statutory powers to give boards directions of a "general character" were regarded as being too blunt. The White Paper believed it to be wrong in principle that a minister could not statutorily intervene in matters of major importance, and consequently suggested that ministers should be given the power to compel the boards of nationalised industries, through the issue of specific directives, to take any action viewed as necessary in the national interest. This new power was seen as likely to improve accountability in that when such a direction was given it would "indicate formally and publicly when the Government had decided to overrule the Board's judgment".

37. Control of the power. The Chief Secretary to the Treasury indicated that the government only intended to use such a power sparingly, and in any case:

(*a*) specific directions would be subject to parliamentary procedures;

(*b*) compensation would be paid to the industries if the directions resulted in loss of money.

38. N.E.D.C. proposals. The National Economic Development Council proposals in this area made in 1976 suggesting the establishment of *policy councils* were rejected in the White Paper. These policy councils would have been established for each industry and would have been composed of representatives of the government, trade unions, management and consumers. The Government in the White Paper rejected the proposal on the grounds that:

(*a*) it would add an additional layer to the administrative structure of the industries without providing clear demarcation lines;

(*b*) industrial boards at present in existence can be widened to include the additional and wider representation suggested, and thus new Policy Councils would be superfluous;

(*c*) part of the functions of the policy councils are achieved by the implementation of the White Paper's recommendations on strengthening of consumer councils, and the extension of industrial democracy within the industries.

39. Commercial and financial proposals. The White Paper outlined the investment, pricing and efficiency policies to be followed to preserve the commercial soundness of the industries and to overcome the "mistakes of the early 1970s" when the prices of public sector goods were held down at the cost of mounting deficits, loss of management morale, etc. The Government clearly intended that the industries would not be forced into deficits by a policy of restraints. To this end the White Paper returned to the philosophy of commercial discipline with regard to investment criteria, pricing policy, and financial targets as established in the 1967 White Paper. The main difference was the incorporation of the concept of required rate of return (R.R.R.) on new investment projects as a whole which replaced the test rate of discount.

On the subject of pricing, the White Paper stated that the government must satisfy itself that the main elements of the industries' pricing structures were sensibly related to the costs of supply and to market conditions. Financial targets would be agreed with each individual enterprise, and tailored to allow for the circumstances of the particular industry.

40. Nature of the public sector. Although the 1978 White Paper returned in many respects to the White Paper of 1967, and in particular the concept of R.R.R. developed within the 1967 principle of general financial objectives, some measure of capital costs which were more related to achieving performance and more even pricing, it must be questioned whether comparatively minor adjustments to the structure were still appropriate. The major factor was that the public sector had shown fundamental changes in the previous decade from the Morrisonian concept of socialised utilities. For example in addition to these utilities and the old nationalised industries such as coal and railways, there was added what may be described as "hybrid" organisations such as British Leyland, Rolls-Royce and Ferranti under the general "tutelage" of the National Enterprise Board. In addition within the public sector had fallen aerospace, shipbuilding and the British National Oil Corporation, together with long standing deviants from the original concept such as B.P. and Harland and Wolff.

PROGRESS TEST 13

1. What are the characteristics of public corporations? What is their significance in public administration? **(1, 2)**

2. Compare the arguments for and against public owner-ship. **(3, 4)**

3. Outline the forms of public ownership. **(5)**

4. Describe in general terms the administrative structure of public corporations. **(6–8)**

5. Comment on the parliamentary supervision of public corpo-rations. What proposals for reform have been made? **(9, 10)**

6. What are the ministries' powers in relation to public corpora-tions? How may such control be interpreted? **(11, 12)**

7. What views did the Select Committee on Nationalised Indus-tries have on ministerial control? **(14–16, 19)**

8. What basic principles did the Select Committee observe? Comment on its distinction between strategic and tactical control. **(17, 18)**

9. What ten principles of control did the Select Committee lay down? **(20)**

10. What are the basic features of the economic and financial position of the public corporations? **(21)**

11. What recommendations were made by the White Paper of 1961? How may these be criticised? **(22, 23)**

12. What recommendations were made by the White Paper of 1967? **(24)**

13. What did the Select Committee observe on the social oblig-ations of the corporations? **(25–27)**

14. Comment on the Select Committee's recommendations for a Ministry of Nationalised Industries. **(28–30)**

15. Why was this suggestion rejected? **(33)**

16. Explain and comment on the proposals in the White Paper of 1978. **(36–40)**

CHAPTER XIV

Judicial Control of Public Administration

INTRODUCTION

The purpose of this chapter is not to present a detailed study of principles of administrative law, but to examine the broad judicial concepts within which the administration functions.

1. Fundamental issues. The overall context of judicial control in the administrative process has been aptly described by Professor S. De Smith (in his *Judicial Review of Administrative Action*, Stevens, 1973) as follows.

"In the broad context of the administrative process the role of judicial institutions is inevitably sporadic and peripheral. The administrative process is not, and cannot be, a succession of justifiable controversies. Public authorities are set up to govern and administer, and if their every act or decision were to be reviewable on unrestricted grounds by an independent judicial body the business of administration could be brought to a standstill. The prospect of judicial relief cannot be held out to every person whose interests may be adversely affected by administrative action."

The following points will be dealt with.

(*a*) There must be established appropriate fields of action for the courts and for the administration.

(*b*) Administrative law must therefore be concerned with judicial aspects of administration and not with policy aspects, though this condition necessarily limits the effectiveness of judicial review.

(*c*) The courts are not concerned with maladministration (but see the role of the Parliamentary Commissioner, **17–18** below).

2. The need for a system of public law. In a completely authoritarian society public law has no application, as every decision by the state consists of the application of administrative discretion. Other opposition to the concept of a division between private and public law has come from legal philosophers such as Duguit and Dicey. The former insisted that complete equality before the law could not be obtained where different bodies of law applied to governors and governed. The latter, also concerned with equality before the law, misinterpreted the role of administrative courts, saying that they were not to provide equality, but to protect the government in its exercise of arbitrary power.

A system of public law is, however, necessary for the following reasons.

(*a*) Government has to govern, and thus complete equality on the basis of the private law system is not practicable.

(*b*) Interference with the activities of private citizens may be a necessary part of the governmental process, but would be prohibited by private law.

3. Public responsibility and private rights. Public law must be concerned with the balance between government responsibility and private rights. British administrative law, however, suffers from the following defects in this respect.

(*a*) Unlike continental systems of public law, which deal with the substance of administrative decisions, definition of the correct sphere of government, etc., British law concentrates almost exclusively on remedies and procedures against public authorities. It thus operates on the circumference of administration rather than becoming an integral checking force therein.

(*b*) The courts have imposed limits on their own province of intervention by their reliance on conceptualising in situations where they have been entitled to exercise discretion, and thus have effectively tied their own hands and made difficult the reversal of past judicial approaches.

(*c*) The absence of special administrative courts in Britain has had the following effects.

(*i*) It has prevented a more coherent and unified development of administrative law.

(*ii*) It has prevented the clear identification of the respective fields of judicial intervention and administrative authority.

(*iii*) It has resulted in a failure to indicate clearly the appropriate boundaries of public law and concepts it exclusively involves.

(*iv*) It has prevented a more adequate definition of the disparities between citizens and the administration.

(*d*) British public law has failed to establish basic principles upon which decisions on the limits of administrative discretion may be taken; i.e. "what is 'arbitrary' and where, consequently, the limits of discretion have to be drawn, depends on the scale of human values as it is enshrined in the contemporary legal system" (W. Friedman, *Law in a Changing Society*, Penguin, 1976). Although not providing a complete answer to all problems of administrative law, an attempt to rationalise the underlying concepts of liberty, etc., would provide a platform and establish a minimum jurisdictional approach.

4. General exemptions from judicial control. The following exemptions should be noted.

(*a*) *Policy areas*. Especially in the international sphere, it is accepted that certain major policy areas are exempt from court interference. Similarly, on a domestic scale, the underlying policy assumptions of administration are not subject to court challenge.

(*b*) *Administration*. "Planning" and "policy-making" decisions of government and other public authorities are not the subject of judicial intervention. In general, this means that the content of policy decisions made by public bodies is not to be the subject of judicial review on its inherent merits. English courts have, however, on occasions limited the effect of complete administrative discretion by construction of the "reasonableness" concept in administrative decisions.

NOTE: Distinction must be made between the exempt "planning" level and the judicially responsible "operational" level.

CROWN PROCEEDINGS

5. Background to the Crown Proceedings Act 1947. Prior to the Crown Proceedings Act 1947, actions against the Crown in contract or tort were severely limited. In both cases, proceedings could only be brought after obtaining a *fiat* by the cumbersome petition of right procedure, and then only on restricted grounds. In tort, petition of right only lay in respect of pure torts, i.e. torts connected with the taking of property; and in contract certain classes were exempt, namely contracts of service with members of the armed forces and Crown servants, contracts which fettered future executive action and contracts dependent on a grant of money from Parliament. In addition certain procedural defects existed in proceedings against the Crown (as typified by the House of Lords decision in *Duncan* v. *Cammel Laird and Company* (1942); *see* **6** (*c*).

The Crown was not vicariously liable for acts of its servants in tort nor was a servant individually liable in contract where the contract was entered into as part of his official duties.

NOTE: A few statutory exceptions existed which permitted actions against the Crown and in practice the Crown would often effectively defend actions by the practice of putting up nominated defendants or paying damages assessed against individual Crown servants. The practice of nominated defendents was, however, subsequently judicially disapproved.

6. Crown Proceedings Act 1947. This dealt with the following matters.

(*a*) *Contract*. British common law has never distinguished between the government contract and the private non-government contract, and consequently has not recognised the inherent difficulties in the application of private law contractual principles to the often completely divorced governmental situation. With this may be compared the French approach which divided government contracts into *contrats administratif* (public law contracts) and *gestions privées* (private law governed) and consequently provides special procedures for government contract administration and compensation of private parties in respect thereof. The British position as a result of s. 1 of the Crown Proceedings Act 1947, in general makes all government contracts judicially enforceable, but exempts those in situations where a petition of right would not have lain before the Act. However, the position is confused by the failure clearly to define the scope of these exemptions and the tendency of the courts in some cases to be guided by considerations of equity and fair play.

The exemptions from liability are as follows.

(*i*) Contracts fettering future executive action are not enforceable. This exemption, however, suffers from lack of clear judicial definition, and in particular from the fact that the two principal cases failed to establish beyond doubt the extent of the exemption In the *Amphitrite* case it was stated that "it cannot by contract hamper its freedom of action in matters concerning the state," whereas Denning's dictum in *Robertson* v. *Minister of Pensions* (1948), was that "it only avails the Crown where there is an implied term to that effect, etc.," and thus the scope of the situation is left open.

(*ii*) Contracts dependent on a grant from Parliament are exempt from enforceability, and thus place long-term major capital works contracting in some uncertainty.

(*iii*) Contracts with Crown servants are legally exempt but in practice little difficulty of unofficial enforcement arises.

NOTE: Provision is not made for compensation in the above cases and represents the British courts' attitude that there is either a common law contract or no contract at all.

(*b*) *Tort*. English law has now recognised the equality of government and governed in this sphere (s. 2(1) Crown Proceedings Act 1947) and renders the Crown generally liable for torts committed by Crown servants in the course of their duties.

(*c*) *Procedural matters*. The proviso to s. 28(1) of the Crown Proceedings Act 1947, preserved the decision of the House of Lords in *Duncan* v. *Cammell Laird and Company* (1942) to the effect that the Crown may refuse to answer questions or produce documents on the ground that it would be contrary to the national interest to do so, and which left the determination of national interest to the appropriate minister. This rule has finally been breached by the subsequent decision of the House in *Conway* v. *Rimmer* (1968) in which it was held that *Duncan* v. *Cammell Laird* had been wrongly interpreted and that the determination of production or non-production on the grounds of national interest was a matter for the courts to decide.

REMEDIES AND PROCEDURES

7. British and continental systems compared. The recognition of a separate administrative law and jurisdiction has in France and Germany been accompanied by a clear and simple form of procedure and remedies. In France an aggrieved individual may file a petition stating his claim in the appropriate administrative court, the grounds upon which he seeks relief, and the relief sought. In Germany there is a similar position involving challenge by petition for nullification and declaration, or for performance. Although *locus standi* (*see* **8**) is required in both jurisdictions this is liberally construed e.g. in France any consumer of a product affected by administrative action is entitled to petition for relief. On the other hand, the common law approaches have been criticised (by K. C. Davies, *Administrative Law*, 1951) for their unnecessary technicality and complexity: "for no practical reason the remedies are plural . . . the lines are moved about through discussions of such concepts as judicial, non-judicial, discretionary and ministerial. These concepts are acutely unfortunate, not only because they defy definition but because of the complete folly of using any concepts whatever to divide one remedy from another."

8. Locus standi. Before consideration of the general nature of judicial remedies and proceedings may be undertaken, it is necessary to examine in outline the situations in which judicial relief may be invoked. In most systems of law judicial remedies may only be invoked by those whose personal interests or rights have been affected by administrative action. There is no equivalent in English law of the *actio popularis* of Roman law, which permitted individuals to bring actions in respect of certain public wrongs. In addition, the right in English law of challenging an act or decision varies in detail between the particular remedies sought. In general, however, two broad approaches may be discerned as follows.

(*a*) The Attorney General may act on his own or at the suit of an individual to enforce duties owed by public authorities. An individual, however, only has *locus standi* in such matters if he has suffered loss different in kind to that suffered by the public at large.

(*b*) Where statutory remedies are provided, it is usual to restrict these to "persons aggrieved". "Persons aggrieved" has never been absolutely defined, but in general has been restricted in meaning to persons who have been deprived of something to which they were legally entitled, or burdened with some obligation wrongfully. It does not cover mere dissatisfaction with a decision or being prejudiced by that decision. As Professor Davis has pointed out: "One whose interests are in fact subjected to or imminently threatened with substantial injury from government action satisfies the requirements of standing and ripeness to challenge the legality of that action unless for reasons of substantive policy the interests are undeserving of legal protection" (Standing, "Ripeness and Civil Liberties." *A.B.A.J.* 1952).

9. Classification of grounds for review. The traditional areas of judicial review exercised through the media of the prerogative orders, injunctions, etc., may be classified as follows.

(a) *Excess of power*. Statutory bodies are subject to the doctrine of *ultra vires*, i.e. they may do only those things which they are expressly or impliedly permitted to do, and those things which are incidental to the performance of such powers. The courts have, however, extended this right to examine for "excess of power" by looking into the jurisdictional facts, i.e. had the inferior body reached its decision by wrongful interpretation of the facts which constitute its jurisdiction? Had discretionary powers been exercised for the purposes for which they were granted? Had the decision been exercised in good faith?

(b) *Procedural defects*. Courts will generally review the way in which a decision was reached, and in particular special emphasis is placed on the rules of natural justice which require that a person whose rights are subject to adjudication is afforded a hearing (though not necessarily oral), and that no man may be judge in his own cause (i.e. there must be no evidence of bias of the adjudicator, though this is construed fairly liberally in administrative matters).

(c) *Error of law*. Courts will intervene where there is evidence that a decision has been taken wrongly in law. Such error of law must, however, appear on the face of the record or documents contemporaneous therewith.

(d) *Reasonableness*. It was held in *Associated Provincial Picture Houses Ltd.* v. *Wednesbury Corporation* (1947) that the decision of a public authority can be upset if it is unreasonable in the sense that no reasonable body could have come to such a decision. This ruling, however, should not be construed too widely and in general some identifiable legal fault in the decision must be established.

10. Remedies. The principle judicial remedies consist of the prerogative orders of *mandamus*, *certiorari* and prohibition, injunctions, declarations and certain specific statutory remedies.

11. The prerogative orders. These are as follows.

(*a*) *Certiorari and prohibition*. These orders are conveniently dealt with together owing to the procedural similarities. The former lies to stop a wrongful action by a public body, whereas the latter lies to bring the decision of an inferior body up for review and to quash that decision if necessary. The basic defect in the remedies, however, is that they will only lie in respect of judicial acts, and not in those cases where the public authority is acting in a purely administrative or ministerial capacity. The concept of the judicial action is itself imprecise and varies according to the particular situation for which the definition is required—and often according to the court's particular designs. However, a decision may be said to be judicial in general terms where the body taking the decision had the trappings of a court, or the action resembled a *lites inter partes*, or where a pronouncement is made on the rights of an individual.

These remedies are principally invoked in cases of *ultra vires*, breach of the rules of natural justice and (in the case of *certiorari*) error of law on the face of the record.

(*b*) *Mandamus*. This lies to enforce a public duty. It cannot be used to enforce discretionary acts but will lie where a discretion is required to be exercised. Generally it only lies at the suit of the Attorney General, though in exceptional cases of interference with private rights an individual may maintain an action.

12. The declaration. The declaratory judgment is becoming the principal remedy of administrative law, owing to its flexibility, its absence of limitation to purely judicial matters, its ability to range widely across administrative matters and its non-coercive nature. It consists of asking the court to declare what the law is in a given case in the event of threatened illegality. It is in practice often coupled with a request for an injunction to restrain the proposed illegality. Owing to its non-coercive nature it is often used to decide disputes between public authorities, and to declare private rights.

NOTE: Statutory appeals are steadily gaining ground as legislative regulation of the administrative process increases.

ORGANISATION OF ADMINISTRATIVE JUSTICE

13. General. Where ordinary courts are not entrusted by the legislature with the settlement of disputes, one of three provisions has generally been adopted:

(a) special (or administrative) tribunals;

(b) ministerial decision following a statutory inquiry, e.g. planning and compulsory purchase appeals;

(c) ministerial decision which is discretionary without prescribed procedure, in which case generally only political redress is open to the citizen.

14. The Franks Report. The present system of administrative tribunals stems largely from the Report of the Committee on Administrative Tribunals and Inquiries (Franks Committee) which formed the basis of the Tribunals and Inquiries Acts of 1958 and 1966. The Committee considered that tribunals should only be resorted to in circumstances where the courts were obviously unsuitable, but that such tribunals should not be treated as mere appendages of government departments. They should be regarded as part of the machinery for adjudication, and not, as official evidence suggested, as part of the machinery for administration. Of particular importance was the rejection by the Committee of Professor Robson's proposal that a General Administrative Appeals Tribunal should be set up to hear appeals from tribunals, as opposed to appeal to the ordinary courts which was ultimately decided upon. The Committee rejected the proposal on the following grounds:

(a) it would not have the expertise of the individual tribunals (this would apply equally to the courts, however);

(b) it would involve departure from the principle that all tribunals should be subject to the supervisory jurisdiction of the High Court;

(c) it could lead to a dichotomy in administrative law decisions.

NOTE: An opportunity was thus lost to establish a body which could have had considerable unifying influence on the development of English public law.

15. Tribunals and Inquiries Acts 1958 and 1966. These are principally a matter for examination in a work on administrative law and it must suffice here to mention some of the more important points.

(a) A Council on Tribunals was set up with a general supervisory role over the administrative tribunals.

(*b*) Machinery for the appointment of members was vested in the Council and the Lord Chancellor and thus kept outside the administrative hierarchy.

(*c*) It was made possible to appeal to the High Court.

(*d*) Reasoned decisions, etc., were required.

16. Exclusion of judicial review. The courts have been reluctant to permit removal of the power of review, and such reluctance is manifested in the principle of statutory construction which prohibits exclusion of recourse to the courts only by the use of clear language. The following general points are worthy of notice.

(*a*) It is possible effectively to exclude review, however, and if effectively carried out there exists no principle by which the validity of a statutory provision itself can be called into question as, for example, by virtue of the "due process" clause of the 5th and 14th Amendments to the Constitution of the U.S.A.

(*b*) The courts, in interpreting statutes purporting to exclude judicial review, construe them liberally in favour of the individual; e.g. the use of the word "final" in a statute does not preclude judicial review but generally only relates to the particular statutory proceedings in question. However, the expression "not to be questioned in any legal proceedings whatsoever" has been held effectively to exclude review (*Smith* v. *East Elloe Rural District Council* (1956)).

(*c*) Where a statute has made a specific remedy available to the person aggrieved by a decision taken under the statute by an administrative agency, the courts will decline jurisdiction to review that decision in other legal proceedings.

17. The Parliamentary Commissioner for Administration. Although not strictly appropriate to a chapter on judicial review, the role of the Parliamentary Commissioner has been included to illustrate how an attempt has been made to deal with the principal area from which the courts are precluded, i.e. that of maladministration. The Parliamentary Commissioner Act 1967, requires the Commissioner to examine and report upon those cases where an individual has "sustained injustice in consequence of maladministration" by certain government departments performing administrative functions, upon reference of the case to him by way of the complainant's M.P.

18. The role and its relation to judicial control. The following points may be made.

(*a*) There are wide exclusions from the Parliamentary Commissioner's ambit including such matters as police, Crown servants' complaints, National Health Service, government contracts, etc. (but *see* 19). These limit the value of the office and also extend the field outside control other than purely political control.

(*b*) The appointment of the Parliamentary Commissioner may be regarded as an indication of the weakness of judicial control, but instead of attempting to strengthen this more effective control the impetus to judicial reform in this field has been weakened by such an appointment.

19. Extension of the system. The concept of the role of the "ombudsman" has now been extended as a result of the appointment of a Health Service Commissioner by the National Health Service Reorganisation Act 1973, and the appointment of local government commissioners by the Local Government Act 1974.

PROGRESS TEST 14

1. Why is there a need for a system of public law?   (**2**)

2. What are the main defects in the English system of public law?   (**3**)

3. What general fields of administration are exempt from judicial control?   (**4**)

4. Outline the provisions of the Crown Proceedings Act 1947. (**6**)

5. Compare the remedies and procedures in English and in continental law. (**7, 8**)

6. What are the basic grounds for judicial review?   (**9**)

7. Describe the principal judicial remedies. (**10, 11, 12**)

8. What were the basic conclusions of the Franks Report on Administrative Tribunals?   (**14**)

9. Comment on the "exclusion" of judicial review.   (**16**)

10. Consider the role of the Parliamentary Commissioner for Administration and his relation to judicial control.   (**17, 18**)

CHAPTER XV

Administration and the Public

PUBLIC OPINION

1. Introduction. Modern concepts of democracy imply that government should not only be representative of the views of the electorate at large but should also be influenced by public opinion between elections, though a precise definition of the extent of such influence is difficult to establish. Such influence may be manifested through pressure groups (*see* **4**), through party machinery (*see* **11**) and through the mass media. In practice, however, this question of expression of public opinion is almost impossible to define or quantify.

2. Problems of definition. The fact that in a democracy an election produces a government which is chosen by the majority of the people is in itself an inadequate safeguard of the public interest, even if it were always a correct assumption. In particular, note the degree of recognition of the interests of particular forms of public opinion, as follows.

(*a*) *Minority opinion.* British government is based at its most fundamental level on respect for the rights of minorities. This respect is both practical, in that governments must pay attention to the views of minorities when faced with fairly regular elections, and based on the principle which prevents the imposition of oppressive measures against minorities. It is thus manifested in the consensus approach of government. In addition, despite broad categories of social class support for the individual parties, each party relies to a considerable extent on a non-class-based vote; e.g. the Conservative party would be unlikely to be elected without a considerable working-class vote, and consequently this multi-class basis of government support in the country prevents the ready identification and oppression of minority interests.

(*b*) *Informed opinion.* The manifestation of public opinion, however, does not relate to numerical support. Informed and articulate opinion has a greater chance of exerting influence on the government as such opinion will tend to monopolise many of the major channels of communication, e.g. industry, the press, political organisations, etc.

(c) *Group opinion* (*see* 4).

3. Manifestation of public opinion. The limitations of the three methods by which it is often suggested that public opinion may make itself felt upon government may be considered as follows.

(a) *Doctrine of the mandate*. This basically involves the issue of whether a government is elected simply to govern or whether it is elected to govern according to particular electorally approved programmes. The issue is clouded in practice by political use made of the idea of the mandate as a justification for unpopular policies, as a means for self-congratulation after the achievement of policies, or as an opposition tool for castigating governments who fail to fulfil their election promises.

By definition, the doctrine implies that a government is bound to carry out those, and only those, policies approved by the electorate at the election which brought it to power. The doctrine is, however, subject to serious limitations as a practical constitutional doctrine.

(i) The multiple and diverse nature of election programmes must result in the impossibility of concluding that every part of the programme has received electoral scrutiny and approval.

(ii) The doctrine is unable to distinguish between ends and means, and thus, whilst theoretically approving broad general political policy, is unable to deal with the methods by which such policy is to be implemented, and which may well alter the end result of the policy.

(iii) It is impossible for precise directions to be given on technical or other complex matters. Without resorting to élitist philosophies it must be doubted whether an unwieldy and technically uneducated electorate as a whole could presume to dictate on certain matters.

(iv) Governments must have the power to deal with unforeseen circumstances and cannot therefore afford in the interests of good government to be tied to rigid programmes.

(v) Similarly, it is doubtful whether such a doctrine could be applied throughout the whole term of a government's office as policy must of necessity change in response to changing circumstances.

(*b*) *Referendum.* It is theoretically possible that a government could govern through public opinion by using the referendum. In practice, however, the administrative difficulties and the time-consuming factors involved would prevent effective decision-making by a government. In addition, it would necessitate, if taken to extremes, the reference of matters to a body not suited to deal with them.

The referendum has however now been employed in relation to Britain's entry into the E.E.C. and is part of the Devolution Bills for Scotland and Wales. It would thus appear that there is a case for the use of referenda where the topic concerned is of fundamental political, constitutional, and social importance. The argument in these cases is that the matters involved go beyond the normal political decision, and consequently public opinion should be expressed on the matter.

(*c*) *Public opinion polls.* The political preoccupation with public opinion polls raises the question of whether they might be utilised effectively as manifestations of public opinion and as such influence governments. This, however, raises two basic questions, namely, whether the polls represent public opinion and, if so, to what extent they should be followed. In addition, the fundamental question as to their accuracy must be borne in mind, and in particular the following points.

(*i*) Persons are given purely hypothetical questions to answer.

(*ii*) Polls may be used (as are by-elections) for the recording of a purely "protest vote".

(*iii*) Although they represent mid-term unpopularity of governments it must be seriously questioned whether governments should be influenced by this or merely rely on long-term approval of their policies (or perhaps, more cynically, on the short memories and apathy of the electorate).

PRESSURE GROUPS

4. Introduction. The normal practice of political representation, being territorial, is supplemented by the functional representation of pressure groups. The methods of testing public opinion dealt with above (*see* **3**) are generally too imprecise to be translatable into concrete policy, and consequently attention must be paid to more direct forms of influence upon government.

Professor R. McKenzie has commented that "pressure groups are more important than political parties for the transmission of political ideas from the mass of the citizenry to their rulers". ("Parties, Pressure Groups, and the British Political Process", *Political Quarterly*, Vol. XXIX, No. 1, 1958.)

5. Definitions. Pressure-group politics has been defined as "the field of organised groups possessing both formal structure and real common interests, in so far as they influence the decisions of public bodies . . . or in so far as they seek to influence the process of government" (McKenzie). Pressure groups in general may be categorised as "defensive" and "promotional" in the following way.

(*a*) *Defensive pressure groups.* These are basically concerned with the protection of their members' interests, and have a defined membership (though such membership in practice often exceeds that of promotional groups). Their membership is not based on any specific sections of the community but ranges from upper-middle-class membership of the Confederation of British Industries to the working-class membership of trade unions. They have been classified by Duverger as "partial", to the extent that they provide service functions for their members as well as under-taking "political" action.

(*b*) *Promotional pressure groups.* These are concerned with promoting some general public interest as opposed to their own self-interest. Although they are theoretically able to call upon a larger membership than the defensive groups, there being no formal limitation on their membership, they in fact tend to have smaller numbers with an essentially middle-class bias. Duverger has also classified them as "exclusive" as in general they offer no service functions to their members.

6. Focus of pressure groups. Although politically orientated, there is little formal affiliation within the pressure group structure, the principal example of affiliation being that of the trade union movement to the Labour party. The focal point of their lobbying tends to be upon the executive and the political parties rather than upon the legislature. This attitude may be explained on the following grounds:

(a) a tradition of contact of pressure groups with M.P.s;

(b) the unitary system of British government and the growing relative importance of the executive;

(c) the position of the executive at operational level;

(d) the tradition of party government in this country which requires M.P.s to serve their party rather than factional interests, as, for example, in the U.S.A.

7. Nature of the relationship between the executive and the pressure group. It is the nature of this relationship which explains the importance of pressure groups in the British system of government as exerters of influence on government and legislation. The expansion of government activity has resulted in a realisation that active co-operation of various groups is necessary in order to achieve effective policy-making and execution of policy. The two-way nature of the relationship may be illustrated as follows.

(a) There has been considerable institutionalisation of pressure groups within the governmental framework as a result of the government's need to consult and to obtain the consent and co-operation of these groups which will be intimately concerned with the operation of government policy, e.g. the importance of the British Medical Association to the operation of the National Health Service.

(b) This recognition has received expression through the machinery of advisory committees, e.g. the Central Advisory Council for Education meets to consider papers prepared by civil servants and to represent the "consumer" view. This committee has in fact produced a series of important reports, viz. Crowther, Newsom, and Plowden, which have been major contributions to educational policy.

(c) The institutionalisation and importance of pressure groups may be regarded as both a duty and a necessity. Such duty may be statutorily recognised, e.g. the Agriculture Act 1947, makes consultation obligatory. Politically, this relationship has been expressed as follows: "It is our duty to consult with the Confederation of British Industries, the Trade Union Congress and others" (H. Wilson, House of Commons Speech, October 1966).

(d) The necessity of consultation has been expressed as follows: "Collectively, one of these organisations knows far more of government policy over a wide field than any individual can hope to attain to". "If firms and other interests were to starve the civil service of . . . the information, the administration of the country would come to a halt" (Blondel, *Voters, Parties, and Leaders*, Pelican, 1969).

(*e*) In addition to formal machinery, considerable informal consultation exists with the group interests.

(*f*) The difficulty of making and implementing policies without pressure-group co-operation has been summed up by Blondel: "The intermixing between outsiders and the civil service has now reached a point where the distinction between 'administrative decisions' and 'decisions taken by private individuals' is more and more difficult and more useless to make".

8. Promotional and exclusive groups. The comments above apply to the defensive groups, the promotional groups not being anything near as institutionalised and having to rely on different access to government than that stemming from the two-way relationship of the defensive groups. In particular, their potentialities for success depend on such factors as the non-political nature of their aims, their ability to influence and win the support of individual M.P.s and the public, party adoption of their aims, etc. Their principal achievements thus lie in the extent they are able to publicise the moral issues with which they are usually concerned.

9. Criticism of group opinion politics. Criticisms levelled at the British system of pressure groups, particularly those of the institutionalised character, are as follows.

(*a*) They may result in unfair advantages being gained by easily organised groups or groups with large memberships and financial resources.

(*b*) There is a tendency within the groups for oligarchies to develop which may be remote from the ordinary membership, and also for the ordinary membership to be subordinated to the groups' paid bureaucracy which effectively controls the policy-making role.

(*c*) It is also often suggested that the sheer power and importance accorded to group interests may operate to pervert the normal processes of government within a democracy. However, in this respect the British system of government provides certain safeguards. In particular, restraints upon the influence of groups are exercised by the representative and responsible nature of

British government, through the responsibility of the executive to the electorate at large, and through the party organisations.

10. Conclusions on group influence. Although not being exhaustive of all interest affected by government activity, such groups do enable the vital process of consultation to be effectively carried out, and thus provide a major exercise in influencing the course of governments.

THE POLITICAL PARTIES

11. Channels of opinion. Political parties may act as channels of opinion from the rank and file to the political leadership in Parliament. However, the degree to which this occurs, and its effectiveness, are difficult to assess. Undoubtedly a government must pay heed to discontent at grass roots level, e.g. the Labour Government's retreat from their proposed Industrial Relations Bill in 1969 in the face of considerable union hostility, though instances of this in practice are not easy to find.

12. Effect of the party conferences. Basically, the Labour and Conservative parties operate from different structural principles. Whereas the Labour party regards itself as a party which has grown upwards, from its local bases, the Conservative party has grown downwards, in the sense that all elements in the party are subordinate to the parliamentary party. In consequence, one would expect to find greater attention paid to membership views in the Labour party than under the absolute political leadership system inherent in the Conservative party. The following points should be noted.

(a) *The Labour Party Conference*. According to Earl Attlee "the Labour Party Conference issues instructions which must be carried out by . . . its representatives in Parliament" (Quoted in R. T. McKenzie, *British Political Parties*, Heinemann, 1963). Theoretically, the Conference has the right "to decide from time to time what specific proposals of legislative, financial or administrative reform shall be included in the party programme if adopted by a majority of not less than two-thirds of the votes recorded on a card vote". In addition, the National Executive Committee may require responsible ministers to appear before its relevant subcommittee where government policy differs from resolutions passed by the Conference. However, this request for explanation is not the same as a power to issue binding instructions.

In practice, the influence is not what Attlee claimed, and in particular the following points should be noted.

(*i*) It is not reconcilable with the true nature of responsible government.

(*ii*) The leader of the parliamentary Labour party is not elected by the conference.

(*iii*) M.P.s usually constitute a majority on the National Executive Committee.

(*iv*) In general, support of the major unions for government policy exists and, even where union support does not exist, constituency support for the parliamentary party compensates.

NOTE: Despite the drawbacks, influence may be exercised by the Conference, though this tends to be exercised after the event and consists of general rather than operational policy influence (*see* V).

(*b*) *The Conservative Party Conference*. The Conference of the National Union is subordinate to the parliamentary party. There is little tendency to attempt to dictate; rather it exists to advance the party cause. In addition, the party bureaucracy is under the control of the party leader.

PARTICIPATION IN THE GOVERNMENTAL PROCESS

13. Fulton Committee. In its *Report* on the civil service, the Fulton Committee emphasised the need for less secrecy in the conduct of the administration, for increased consultation and for greater public participation in the policy-planning process. Of particular importance, it disagreed with the oft-quoted bureaucratic view that increased participation would lead to slowness and inefficiency in the decision-making process, believing, in fact, that less secrecy would result in more effective and acceptable decisions being made.

14. Participation. "Participation in the process of planning our inbuilt and natural environment, and the services which affect every individual and family, is the key to successful policy-making and implementation. At present the whole machinery of government is geared to a sequence which begins with the identification of a problem in a central government department, goes on through research conducted centrally or commissioned, and then evaluated behind closed doors, and ends in the announcement, from London, of a decision. The whole system is essentially paternalistic and centralist, with only the most exiguous scope for local variations from the central rules" (*People, Participation and Government, Fabian Research Series* 293, published by the Fabian Society).

The present process of decision-making is thus defective in the following respects.

(*a*) Its over-centralisation effectively prevents both public participation and recognition of local needs.

(*b*) Its conduct is invariably secret.

(*c*) Consultation is effectively limited to certain institutionalised groups (*see* **4**).

(*d*) Government fails to communicate its policies to the people by virtue of its failure or reluctance to use the existing channels of communication, though ostensibly because of the technicality of much of the subject-matter.

(*e*) Ultimately this failure to involve the governed results in a decline in respect for government.

15. Problems of participation. Unrestricted participation in the process of government, however, raises the following problems.

(*a*) There are certain aspects of government policy which of necessity must be conducted in secret, e.g. in the field of economic and fiscal policy-making, participation in which would seriously hinder the process of government. However, it is necessary here to distinguish between participation which would effectively inhibit the government and that which would merely cause administrative inconvenience, and it is important that participation should not be prevented on the latter ground.

(*b*) The problem of the conflict between efficiency and democracy is raised by participation. The nature of governmental activities and the large sums of money involved place a duty on the government to exercise its functions with the greatest efficiency. However, undue extension of the participative process could lead to an extension of the time of administrative decision-making, tendencies to preserve the *status quo* and the down-playing of technical and administrative skills.

(c) Extension of participation could be undesirable in that it would favour the more articulate and politically organised sections of the community to the detriment of those in the positions of greatest social and economic need. Consequently, unless real safeguards were built into the system, the process of participation could result in a widening of social and economic disparities.

16. Possibilities of structural reforms. The possibility of offering participation through the existing machinery of government or through adaptations therein may be considered. The possibilities essentially involve placing decision-making powers closer to the governed in the following ways:

(a) administrative deconcentration involving the decentralisation of decision-making personnel of government departments and not those only exercising mere administration functions;

(b) regionalism of local government with a federalist approach adopted towards the type of powers devolved upon the regions;

(c) effective and accessible local government units within these regions.

17. Conclusion. This subject of participation is one which has been to a large extent ignored by political and public administration theorists, though it is one which goes to the root of effective and democratic public administration. In conclusion the *Fabian Research Pamphlet* referred to above (*see* **14**) made certain valuable suggestions. It considered firstly a series of tests against which an effective participative system of government could be measured, as follows.

(a) Does the general array of authorities allow public services to be administered on a scale both efficient and amenable to local control?

(b) Are decision-making bodies so constituted as to be obliged both to need public approval for their policies and to evolve their policies in a process of continuous consultation?

(c) Are the rights of consumers guaranteed in the constitution of the bodies concerned?

(d) Does the machinery provide for the statutory representation of disadvantaged minorities within the decision-making process?

(e) Is machinery available for review and appeal which is so designed at the same time to prevent delay of implementation of plans and legislation?

(*f*) Is it so designed that no special interests can by-pass or seriously delay the process of government?

In reply to these principles the pamphlet made the following general points:

(*a*) There is a need for fewer statutory levels of government but for more tiers for specialised purposes, e.g. regional councils.

(*b*) At the lower level there is a need for immediately accessible units.

(*c*) There must be institutionalisation at all levels of government of bodies set up to represent minority rights and interests.

PROGRESS TEST 15

1. What meanings may be given to "public opinion"? How may such opinion be manifested? (**2, 3**)

2. Consider the definition of pressure groups. (**4, 5**)

3. Where and why are pressure groups focused in Britain? (**6, 8**)

4. Consider the relationship of the executive and pressure groups. (**7**)

5. What comments may be made on group politics? (**9, 10**)

6. What effects do political parties have as channels of opinion? (**11, 12**)

7. Why is participation in the government process necessary? (**13, 14**)

8. What are the problems of participation? (**15**)

9. How may participation be achieved? (**16, 17**)

CHAPTER XVI

Management Aids and Public Administration

INTRODUCTION

1. Management problems. The Plowden Committee on the Control of Public Expenditure defined management as "the preparation of material on which decisions are taken; the technical efficiency with which large operations of administration are carried out; the cost-consciousness of staff at all levels; the provisions of special skills and services (scientific, statistical, accountancy, O. and M., etc.,) for handling particular problems and the awareness and effectiveness with which they are used; and the training and selection of men and women for posts at each level of responsibility".

This statement may be analysed into distinctive but co-related management functions to which specific management aids may be applied:

(a) planning and decision-making;
(b) control of operational efficiency;
(c) organisation for efficiency;
(d) manpower considerations;
(e) follow-up and feed-back;
(f) information requirements.

2. Management services and techniques. Distinction is usually made between management services and management techniques. The difference generally turns on the fact that the former essentially involve aids to management in the wider sense, e.g. automatic data processing, computers, job evaluation, whereas the latter may be regarded as individual sciences and tools which offer specific solutions to individual problems, e.g. cost benefit analysis, work study, network analysis. This chapter will not, however, dwell on such distinctions but will collectively approach the subject as one of management aids, which will be dealt with according to their relevance to the particular management areas outlined above (*see* 1).

3. Constraints in general on the use of management aids. The particular constraints involved in the use of specific aids will be dealt with as they arise in the text. However, certain general constraints should be observed as follows.

(*a*) *Objectives.* Unlike the business context, management aids cannot always be applied on a straightforward profit maximisation basis in public administration. The need to balance the often competing concepts of democracy and efficiency in itself constrains maximum use of techniques. There is thus an underlying necessity for careful definition of objectives and the operation of the aids within the social and political constraints involved.

NOTE: Given, however, the establishment of objectives, there is no reason why efficiency may not be maximised therein by the use of aids.

(*b*) *Social aspects.* Management aids which involve changing methods and procedures in order to improve efficiency cannot be applied in a vacuum. Such changes have effects on employees and there is a need to realise that ultimate efficiency as an organisational objective may conflict with individual objectives and values. In consequence, a purely mechanistic approach to organisational reform must be balanced against an organic approach which takes account of the social environment, both internal and external, of the organisation.

(*c*) *Personnel constraints.* The effective use of management aids depends on the education of specialised personnel, their appointment to positions of authority in the organisation, and their continued specialist training. The problems connected with the use of such specialists is dealt with in VI.

NOTE: In general, more effective use is made of such specialists in local government than in central government.

COMPUTERS

4. Basic uses. The operation of many management techniques depends on effective utilisation of computers in assistance. In addition, computers in themselves perform valuable functions in control and feedback systems and in information systems.

Computers essentially provide better information for use in co-ordination techniques, and are capable of producing more comprehensive controlling and information retrieval systems.

The unique services provided by computer use may be classified as follows:

(a) speed of operation;
(b) ability to store and retrieve information;
(c) ability to handle large and complicated information;
(d) facility for calculation.

They thus have particular value in complicated and repetitive situations, as centralised control points in organisations, as assistance to individual techniques, e.g. operational research, as central information systems and in the provision of more and reliable information upon which decisions may be made.

5. Some effects of computer use. The following points should be noted.

(a) They reduce the need for some levels of middle and lower management owing to their speed in calculation and communication.

(b) They permit the changeover from scientific management based on functional specialisation to management based on integration of functions.

(c) They have both centralising and decentralising tendencies. They tend to cause a central movement in organisations in respect of repetitive and routine tasks, while providing opportunities for decentralisation of executive functions which may be controlled and co-ordinated by access to the central data bank.

DECISION-MAKING TECHNIQUES

6. Operational research (O.R.). This has been defined as "the application of scientific processes to operational problems arising within organisations, the objectives being to make more effective use of known facts, to enlarge the proportion of factual knowledge and to reduce the proportion of subjective judgment in making management decisions" (*Glossary of Management Techniques*, H.M.S.O., 1967).

The object of O.R. is the establishment of optimum solutions to organisational problems; it involves the application of many tools founded in mathematical statistics. In practice, it operates as follows.

(a) A precise definition of problems in the context of the organisation's objectives is established.

(b) Measurement of relevant factors is undertaken. In the public administration context, the existence of unquantifiable factors is taken account of and in general sufficient statistics are collated in order to permit a gamble on these factors.

(c) A mathematical model is built.

(d) Information flow is established to describe the operation of the system and its divergence from the chosen system.

7. Uses of O.R. In general terms, O.R. techniques have normally been used in the context of business profitability. However, they have also proved of value in the public administration context, where it is necessary to review multiple choices involving generally unquantifiable or unknown factors. Specific examples of the use of O.R. lie in work carried out by the Local Government Operational Research Unit and include such matters as population forecasting, design of financial planning models, planning urban growth, joint refuse disposal problems and research into purchasing methods.

8. Cost benefit analysis (C.B.A.). This has been defined as "a systematic comparison between the cost of carrying out a service or activity and the value of that service or activity, quantified as far as possible, all costs and benefits (direct and indirect, financial and social) being taken into account" (*Glossary of Management Techniques*, H.M.S.O., 1967).

It thus exceeds the normal accounting analysis involving inflows and outflows of cash and attempts to cover all the effects of a proposed project in quantified terms. The basic procedure of C.B.A. is firstly to analyse the primary costs (or direct costs) of a project and the benefits thereof, and then to predict and quantify the indirect costs and benefits (including social factors). These are then evaluated on a common basis.

9. Uses of C.B.A. C.B.A. is of particular value in the public context where administrative choices cannot be guided purely by economic factors, or where social factors predominate. Although certain difficulties arise in its application e.g. the measurement of intangible costs and benefits, or where the reviewed projects contain different intangibles) the process is of value in decision-making in that it involves detailed consideration and comparison of alternative courses of action. In particular, it is of value in reducing to statistical terms matters which would otherwise be the subject of unscientific value judgments.

Noted applications of C.B.A. have been afforded by the Beeching and Buchanan Transportation Studies, the Victoria Line analysis, the M1 analysis and the Roskill Commission on the third London airport. Analyses on a local level have also been carried out and include such matters as alternative methods of staff training, low or high rise housing development and provision of longer runways for airports.

10. Discounted cash flow. Discounted cash flow is a form of investment appraisal of value where long-term investment decisions have to be made. It aims to provide a comparable rate of return against which the investment in various projects may be measured. In particular, it has the following aims:

(*a*) to ensure that investment takes place in those matters providing the highest rate of return;

(*b*) to ensure that investments are not made in projects that will provide a rate of return less than the cost of the capital employed in the business.

It thus provides a method of rationalising investment decisions which illustrates capital locked up in projects and the comparative cash flows therefrom. Although of great value in a business context, its value in public administration must be seen in the light of the various non-commercial factors motivating public investment, e.g. political and social considerations.

11. P.P.B. Formally the aims of "planning, programming and budgeting" have been described as follows:

(*a*) the identification of the objectives of areas of government activity;

(*b*) the identification of activities contributing to such objectives;

(*c*) the measurement of the costs of resources devoted to those activities;

(*d*) the assessment of the results of the various activities.

(Memo on Output Budgeting by Treasury submitted to Select Committee on Procedure).

The object of the approach is to increase rationality in government policy planning. The difference in accounting terms between this approach and traditional expenditure planning is that it relates expenditure to outputs and objectives, and not to inputs or the resources used by the organisation. If the costs of a department's programmes are known it is possible to evaluate the effectiveness of alternative policies leading to the same objectives, and to compare real demands on resources being made by different objectives (the concept of functional costs).

The procedure has been used by the Ministry of Defence to improve their evaluation of the resources used in individual programmes related to broad defence objectives, and by the Home Office in costing how individual policemen contribute to different programmes, and it has shown very different patterns of expenditure from those obtained by conventional accounting methods.

Its major problems are that it is often difficult to devise objective criteria of efficiency, it is difficult to identify costs relating to different parts of a programme, and there are problems of functional overlap where more than one department contributed to programmes in a particular area.

12. Management by objectives. Management by objectives involves the establishment of organisation objectives and the measurement of performance against such objectives. Its use in the public context may prove valuable in those situations where the profit objective is not appropriate. The advantages of formally setting out objectives are as follows:

(*a*) the risks of misunderstanding and of pursuing non-relevant ends are avoided;

(*b*) they are based on forecasting and consequently lessen the chances of future deviation from the overall objectives of the organisation;

(*c*) they provide criteria for assessing overall performance.

CONTROL

13. Network analysis. Network analysis is in fact a technique that could be included under either planning or control, though here it is treated as a control exercise to distinguish it from pure decision-making aids. It has been defined as "methods of planning the undertaking of a complex project in a logical way by analysing the project into component parts and recording them on a network model or diagram which is then used for planning and controlling the inter-related activities in carrying the project to completion" (*Glossary of Management Techniques*, H.M.S.O., 1967).

The object of network analysis is to enable non-standardised projects to be studied over the whole course of their operation, and to estimate the impact of time on the varying factors involved in the achievement of the final goal. In doing this, it highlights the critical steps, the successful completion of which controls the whole project, and provides controlling action thereby.

14. Critical path analysis. This is based on network analysis and operates to distinguish the longest and therefore crucial parts of a project which consequently control the overall completion time. It thus establishes the matters upon which effort must be concentrated, as distinguished from parts which have floating time and thus can be advanced or retarded without affecting the overall programme.

15. Uses of critical path analysis and network analysis. These techniques have valuable control functions both at the planning stage of a project, in that they enable all departments involved to establish clearly their respective functions and responsibilities towards the overall objective, and in the operational stage, where the overall project controller is able to survey the course of the whole operation and pinpoint its weaknesses, establish points of delay, speed up necessary activities, etc.

The techniques are of value in major complex undertakings and are often employed in conjunction with a computer (this is essential in multi-dimensional projects). In the public sector they have been used to great advantage by the U.K. Atomic Energy Authority in reducing tooling time of uranium fuel plants, and consequently improving the ability to meet production schedules and to utilise plant fully. In local government they have principally been used on the technical side of highways, school building, housing and engineering projects. Their application is not limited, however, to technical applications, e.g. they were used to establish new monthly accounting procedures by Colgate-Palmolive Ltd.

16. Other control techniques. The following techniques should be noted.

(*a*) *Management accounting.* This again represents a combined planning and controlling exercise. It involves the application of accounting knowledge and procedures to interpret the statistical information necessary for promotion of maximum efficiency by management in the form of future planning and co-ordination of policy.

(*b*) *Budgetary control.* This has been defined as "allocating financial limits to component parts of individual enterprises and accounting for outlays in such a way as to provide comparisons between actual and forecast results so that, if remedial action is necessary, it may be taken at an early stage or alternatively that overall objectives may be reviewed".

ORGANISATION FOR EFFICIENCY

17. Organisation and methods (O. and M.). O. and M. originated in public administration in the Treasury, though all major departments now have O. and M. sections. It has been defined by the O. and M. Society Constitution as follows:

". . . an advisory service to management and its purpose is:

(*a*) to advise on the most effective organisation for controlling and co-ordinating the administrative elements of the various functions of the business or undertaking;

(*b*) to advise on the detailed methods and procedures to enable those functions to be operated with maximum effectiveness;

(*c*) to ensure that changes in organisation and/or methods which have been agreed are properly implemented."

The object is thus to examine both organisations and the methods employed therein and to eliminate inefficiency, duplication, waste, etc., arising as a result of an organisation failing to adapt to changing circumstances in such matters as the objectives of the organisation, its overall environment, etc.

18. Use of O. and M. The utility of O. and M. is dependent on certain factors, the most important of which are adequate discussion with staff representatives, management support and independence of the O. and M. department from sections of the organisation reviewed.

It has been used in recent years to a considerable extent in local government, in particular, to review the organisation and operational effectiveness of individual departments.

19. Work study. This involves detailed and systematic examination by use of a set of formal techniques and guides into an organisation's work procedures in order to maximise the efficiency of such procedures. In itself, work study is a generic concept embracing such techniques as method study, work measurement and job evaluation. Method study involves the determination of how work should be carried out in the light of current technology, work measurement involves measuring time/effort factors in performing a job within established working conditions and methods and job evaluation involves determining how much work is worth in terms of its mental and physical demands.

20. Other organisational techniques. The following techniques should be noted.

(a) *Ergonomics.* ("The study of the effect of the working environment on the worker and his productive capacity, and the application of anatomical, physiological, and psychological knowledge to the problems arising thereunder" (*Glossary of Management Techniques*, H.M.S.O., 1967).

(b) *Systems analysis.* This involves examination of the organisation with a view to reorganisation, in order to facilitate the carrying out of work by computer.

MANPOWER

21. Job evaluation (*See* **19.**)

22. Management development. There is a growing recognition in the public service of the importance of management development, both in training in use of management skill and in the use of specific techniques. Management development needs to be orientated towards taking advantage of these.

23. Job description. The importance of specifying responsibilities has been dealt with in III.

INFORMATION REQUIREMENTS

24. Nature. An executive's range of competence is related directly to his available supply of information. "A good information system must furnish knowledge that is material to the manager's job, that can be weighed against the goals; it must be designed to determine how and where goals are being missed. It must furnish intelligible data" (Koontz and O'Donnell, *Principles of Management*, McGraw-Hill, 1976).

25. Particular aspects. In establishing information systems within an organisation the following points must be observed.

(*a*) The information system acts both as a planning technique and as a control technique during the operations.

(*b*) The use of the computer greatly facilitates the development of information systems but its use must be selective. The very ability of a computer to assimilate a large amount of information can place undue burdens upon individual managers and consequently there must be a selective approach and discrimination in that information which management requires.

(*c*) Information required by management covers financial, logistic and personnel matters.

26. The systems approach to organisation. The establishment of effective information systems depends not only on individual techniques of computer usage and new accounting procedures, but may be achieved through the design of the organisation itself. This latter approach is favoured by those advocating the systems approach to management (*see* III). It emphasises the necessity of a planned management information system that gives each level of management the appropriate information at the appropriate time.

PROGRESS TEST 16

1. What are the main areas involving management problems found in public administration?   **(1)**

2. What are the principal constraints on the utilisation of management aids in public administration?   **(3)**

3. Consider the basic uses of computers and some effects of computer usage.   **(4, 5)**

4. What is operational research? Of what use is it in public administration?   **(6, 7)**

5. Define cost benefit analysis and give examples of its uses in public projects.   **(8, 9)**

6. Define network analysis and critical path analysis and give examples of their uses in public administration. **(13–15)**

7. Of what value are organisation and methods and work study in public administration? **(18, 19)**

8. What factors must be considered in establishing information systems? **(24, 25)**

CHAPTER XVII

Management in Local Government

TRADITIONAL STRUCTURE AND PRINCIPLES

1. Introduction. The traditional management structure of local government is based on nineteenth-century concepts of democratic control and involves the interplay of councillors, committees and officers. In theory, the council is primarily responsible for policy and for holding the balance between individual departments and committees. The committees themselves are concerned with the detailed consideration of various aspects of local authority work, and formulate proposals for submission to the council. They also act as the link between elected members and paid officers and are engaged in the control and supervision of departments of the council. The officers are primarily concerned with execution of policy decisions, but owing to their position as operators they are also in the best position to give advice on questions of policy and practice.

NOTE: The fundamental concept of local authority management is based, therefore, on the theoretical distinction between policy and administration which is not realistic in the light of modern administration.

2. Co-ordination problems. The practice of dividing functions and the consequent functional specialisation leads to "departmentalism" and thus tends to result in a lack of unity in local authority administration. This has an attendant absence of corporate responsibility which develops isolationist attitudes. In addition, the position is worsened by the inadequacy of the present formal methods of co-ordination, i.e. by way of general purpose committees, finance committees, joint co-ordinative committees and formal definition of functions by the council. This results in the necessary development of informal machinery for co-ordination through committee chairmen, officers, committee clerks and political party machinery.

3. Delegation to officers. The traditional practice of delegation to officers in local authorities is based on the false dichotomy between policy and administration. Compared to the practice in many foreign systems, with general delegation of day-to-day administrative functions to officers and a reserve of major issues to the elected members, English local government is preoccupied with its attitude to democratic control. Democratic control in the English local government context, however, implies detailed control and, instead of permitting full delegation with checks and balances, the English approach misuses officers through its insistence on the reference of all but the most minor matters to committee or council authorisation.

4. Departmental organisation. The English practice of a functional department supported by a matching committee tends to lead to an excessive array of departments which often prove unwieldy or even superfluous and pose serious problems of co-ordination. In addition, co-ordination problems are increased both by the tendency to subdivide too for functions and the failure to establish any recognised hierarchy amongst principal officers.

5. Lack of head of administration and managing body. A further traditional defect of English local government was the absence of a recognised head of administration. Although this position was often accorded to the clerk of the council, his position was generally one of influence rather than control and it was rare for such a post to develop into that of recognised administrative leadership.

In addition, the creation of a central, unified managing body was generally prevented in local government by the practice of delegating management functions to individual committees, thus preventing the development of a focal point of management.

6. The requirements of management. T. G. Thomson (writing in the *Local Government Chronicle*) has suggested, amongst others, that the following principles of management organisation might be followed to considerable advantage in local government.

(*a*) The member structure within a policy committee should be concerned with setting objectives and allocating resources.

(*b*) Executive committees should be based on functional groupings to direct management of these functions.

(*c*) The officer structure should mirror the member structure, with a chief executive officer and functional groupings culminating in a chief executive officer's programming committee.

(*d*) The chief executive officer requires certain supporting machinery namely:

(*i*) to review objectives, test service effectiveness and to provide committees with relevant facts and courses of action open to them;

(*ii*) to deal with internal administration.

(*e*) Financial advisers should have two supporting wings, namely:

(*i*) to deal with financial appraisal and analysis;

(*ii*) to deal with exchequer and historical accounting.

At the conclusion of the chapter the degree to which these principles have been successfully applied will be evaluated (*see* **21**).

THE MAUD COMMITTEE ON MANAGEMENT AND THE REDCLIFFE-MAUD COMMISSION

7. The Maud Committee's conclusions. The Committee made the following general observations on the local government management pattern.

(*a*) It had its roots in nineteenth-century traditions of direct and detailed responsibility. This was necessary and relevant where the range of services provided was limited, where government involvement was minimal and where there were few professional staff. These factors had changed and had consequently removed the fundamental basis of the traditional approach to local government management.

(*b*) A distinction must be drawn between deliberative functions of committee and administrative functions. The then current tendency to exercise detailed administrative functions presents certain marked disadvantages, for the following reasons.

(*i*) Supervision is not practicable owing to constraints of time, technical complexity, etc.

(*ii*) It does not encourage discrimination between major objectives and consequential decisions and actions.

(*iii*) It discourages delegation to officers.

8. Proposals made for reform. The following proposals were made.

(*a*) *Members and officers.* A greater role should be given to officers in day-to-day administration, identification of problems and the provision of staff work necessary to enable members to decide objectives, etc. However, members should have the ultimate direction and control of the affairs of the authority, should take key decisions and should review periodically the programme and performance of services.

(*b*) *Central management.* Local authorities should establish a management board composed of five to nine council members with the following functions:

(*i*) formulation of objectives and means of attainment for presentation to the council;

(*ii*) review of programmes on council's behalf;

(*iii*) maintenance of overall supervision of authority's organisation, co-ordination and integration;

(*iv*) Decision-making of certain kinds on behalf of the council;

(*v*) taking responsibility for presentation of business to the council.

(*c*) *Committees.* The following recommendations were made:

(*i*) committees should be deliberative not directive;

(*ii*) they should not exceed fifteen members;

(*iii*) their functions should consist of making recommendations to the management board, reviewing individual programmes, considering public reaction and conveying this to the council, etc., considering matters raised by their own members or by the management board;

(*iv*) there should be a drastic reduction in the number of committees.

NOTE: They should only take executive decisions when requested by the management board and under the board's strict supervision.

(*d*) *Central official.* The Committee considered that there should be a recognised head officer responsible to the management board, through whom other principal officers would be responsible to the council. He should be responsible for organisation and efficiency, implementing effective control systems, etc.

(e) *Principal officers*. They should work as a team, provide staff work, etc. and would be responsible, through the chief official, to the council for the running of their departments.

9. Note of dissent. Sir Oliver Wheatley dissented from the majority recommendations of the Maud Committee on the basic ground that they would vest too much authority in a small body of members. He consequently suggested that committees should continue to possess executive power and that there should be direct access of committees to the council.

10. The views of the Redcliffe-Maud Commission. The Redcliffe-Maud Commission basically accepted the recommendations of the Maud Committee in regard to the creation of a central committee, the delegation of executive functions to officers and the formation of a team of chief officers as a central management group. In particular, it made the following comments.

(a) *Central board*. The size of local organisational structure, even allowing for maximum use of management techniques, presented difficulties of co-ordination. A central committee or board would provide a focal centre which could transcend departmental interests. It should be concerned with advising the council on strategy and priorities, co-ordinating policies and the work of the service committees and ensuring the application of management techniques.

(b) *Committees*. The nature of local government work effectively limits the degree possible or desirable, and thus there must be a number of committees working with the central committee, such committees making recommendations to the council on general policy and on the specific services under their control.

(c) *Delegation*. This must be more extensive in regard to executive functions. If adequately implemented it would leave councillors more time to exercise their proper functions of control and scrutiny.

CHIEF EXECUTIVE OFFICERS AND THE CITY MANAGER CONCEPT

11. Chief executive officer. The evidence given to the Maud Committee by the Management Consultants Association recommended that there should be one officer in overall administrative authority and ultimately responsible to the council for anything entrusted to the officer body. Each principal officer would be responsible to him for the internal administration of his department. He in turn would be responsible to the council for implementation of council policy, establishment matters, etc., and for co-ordinating the work of departments.

12. The American city manager concept. In broad terms, the American city manager concept involves a small elected council (usually nine or less members), preferably elected on a non-party basis, which makes by-laws, decides the extent and pattern of activities, passes the budget and appoints the manager. The manager has all executive functions delegated to him. These will include appointment and dismissal of departmental heads, framing the budget and controlling the administration and the initiation of policy. He has thus been described as "the hedge between politics and administration, but he is not a politician himself" (Vol. 4 of Maud Committee on Management of Local Government, 1967). In general, managers attempt to operate on commercial management lines, and tend to co-ordinate and direct departments rather than to exercise departmental functions in their own right.

13. Advantages of the system. These are as follows.

(*a*) Professional skill and experience may increase interest in local affairs.

(*b*) The appointment encourages members to concentrate on policy, and thus goes at least part-way to the solution of the problem of marrying public control with efficiency.

(*c*) There are advantages if integrated management accrues namely:

　(*i*) a sense of corporate responsibility is developed;

　(*ii*) officers' views are brought into play at an early stage in policy formation;

　(*iii*) business is more rapidly executed;

　(*iv*) the manager provides a focal point for those dealing with the local authority;

　(*v*) his position is well placed for checking unnecessary departmental growth and for the introduction of management techniques, etc.

14. Disadvantages of the system. These are as follows.

(*a*) In practice it has been found only to be workable in small to middle-sized, relatively homogeneous, communities.

(*b*) It tends markedly to underrate the political aspects of local government.

(*c*) Current management thinking has emphasised the disadvantages of concentrating authority in a single individual (*see* III).

(*d*) It greatly underestimates the possibility in practice of distinguishing between policy and administration functions.

(*e*) There is increased danger of domination being achieved by either the manager or the elected members.

(*f*) Too great a dependence is placed on personalities.

(*g*) In terms of economy in operation of services, it has proved a success. Its effect in communities where there are considerable differences as to the principles of what is to be provided, however, has not been effectively tested.

15. Inappropriateness to English local government. The system is not appropriate for incorporation into the English context of local government, for the following reasons.

(*a*) The political nature of English local government would not provide the proper basis for its adoption.

(*b*) The committee system which is at the basis of the English system would be destroyed.

(*c*) It would necessitate the interlocking of the administrative structure of local government with the political structure of society.

(*d*) In general, the much wider range of services administered by an English local authority would impose considerable strain on a single individual.

(*e*) The reorganisation in 1974 into larger authorities effectively places local authorities outside what has proved to be the appropriate size for the operation of the city manager approach in the U.S.A.

16. Other North American systems. In addition to the city manager concept, the following North American approaches may be appropriately mentioned as being of comparative interest.

(*a*) *Commission government.* This consists of an elected mayor and full-time commissioners, each commissioner specially elected as head of a group of functions.

It has certain advantages:

(*i*) it is not so dependent on personalities as a "one-man" system;

(*ii*) it involves direction by full-time political executives;

(*iii*) it avoids delay in that it combines both political and executive authority;

(*iv*) it increases electoral interest.

Its disadvantages, however, are as follows:

(*v*) while it combines executive and legislative responsibility, it lacks the critical revision process of the English committee system;

(*vi*) its theoretical corporate responsibility is rarely matched in practice by harmony between the commissioners;

(*vii*) it tends to place little emphasis on forward planning;

(*viii*) in concentrating on a political and administrative approach, such matters as up-to-date personnel functions are neglected.

(*b*) *Strong mayor system.* The characteristics generally associated with this system are a politically elected council of five to fifteen members which acts as the legislative body, plus an elected mayor holding office for a two- to four-year term. The mayor prepares the budget and exercises full executive responsibility subject to the council's right to exercise delaying tactics or outright rejection of his policies. Committees are not a necessary part of the system but, where existing, function as sifters of material, etc. The mayor's powerful position rests both on his electoral mandate and his power as chief executive.

Legislative and executive co-ordination depend on various factors including the mayor's personality, party machinery and outside citizens' organisations.

Its advantages are as follows:

(*i*) it places at the head of administration a dynamic personality able to influence opinion, etc.;

(*ii*) it combines political and administrative authority;

(*iii*) according to American beliefs, it is closest to the people.

Against these merits must be set the following disadvantages:

(*iv*) that a political executive tends to lack technical expertise;

(*v*) political debts may be owed to sections of the electorate;
(*vi*) delays between policy formulation and implementation;
(*vii*) it is inadequate for the size of the job.

17. Problems of the chief executive officer. The principal functions
of a chief executive officer may be regarded as co-ordination of
the authority's activities and positive leadership, involving the
bringing forward of new organisational ideas and policies. Problems which must be overcome in order to achieve these objectives
include the following:

(*a*) the dangers and disadvantages of over-emphasis on individual powers and the centralising process;
(*b*) retention of the goodwill of members and other officers;
(*c*) establishment of effective relations with the authority's
policy committee;
(*d*) the establishment of effective lines of communication;
(*e*) a clear definition of the respective roles of committees, chief
officers and departments.

REFORM

18. Developments in the counties. Research carried out subsequent to the Maud Committee *Report* showed the following
developments.

(*a*) *Management boards*. The concept of the management board
was rejected by forty-three counties, for reasons including the
feeling that it was undemocratic, that it deterred the attraction of
suitable members and that members were incapable of absorbing
the necessary amount of work related to membership of the board.

(*b*) *Central committees*. However, twenty-three authorities
established a central committee with clear responsibility for co-
ordination. In nine cases the central co-ordination committee was
also the finance committee, and in fourteen cases separate policy
and finance committees were established.

(*c*) *Committees*. In general, there was a reluctance to prune
committees to the number recommended by Maud. Maud
recommended six, but the county average was nineteen, plus in
some cases thirty or more sub-committees. There was also reluctance to prune committee membership.

(*d*) *Chief executive officer*. Little interest was shown in the chief
executive officer concept, but although delegation was not carried

out to the extent recommended by Maud, there has been reappraisal and reallocation.

THE BAINS REPORT

19. Introduction. The Study Group on Local Authority Management Structures was set up in May 1971 to produce advice for the new local authorities on management structures at both member and officer level. In 1972 it produced its report *The New Local Authorities: Management and Structure*, generally referred to as the Bains Report (*see* also V, **20**).

The report is of particular significance in the development of management organisation in local authorities as most of its major recommendations have been adopted, though often with variations, by the new local authorities.

20. Nature of local authority management. The Bains Report considered that the basic problems exisiting in the management organisation of local government were:

(*a*) the dual nature of management consisting of elected members and officers both exercising "management functions", and thus involving friction and competition, resulting in a loss of efficiency;

(*b*) the traditional departmental attitude.

Its fundamental observation was that the old structure needed to be replaced by one which fostered a "corporate management" approach to local authority organisation, viz. a structure which supported the achievement of overall local authority objectives and in which the member and officer structure was designed to contribute to the achievement of such goals.

21. The role of officers and elected members. The Bains Report made the following observations:

(*a*) neither members nor officers should regard any area of local authority administration as their exclusive preserve;

(*b*) the formulation of policy is not the exclusive preserve of a central policy committee, and, in many cases, it is appropriate for other committees to formulate policy;

(*c*) greater attention must be given to methods of assessing effectiveness against defined objectives resulting from the establishment of an overall plan of objectives;

(*d*) whilst recognising the desirability of the "professional" base of the officer structure dangers arose if this was carried to extreme.

22. Organisational implications of the members' role.

(*a*) The *council* is not to be a mere decision-taking body, but should be involved in policy formulation and as a debating chamber.

(*b*) A *policy and resources committee* should be established with the function of providing co-ordinated advice to the Council in setting plans, objectives and priorities. It should also exercise control over the major resources of the authority, and control and co-ordinate the implementation of the council's programmes.

(*c*) Control over resources should be exercised through the media of three sub-committees. These *resource sub-committees* should exercise day-to-day control over personnel, finance and land.

(*d*) A fourth sub-committee should be established charged with *performance review*.

(*e*) The committee structure should be rationalised and there should be a move from committees linked to individual services to links with areas of the council's overall objectives. These would be regarded as *programme committees*.

23. Organisation at officer level. The Bains Report gave little stress to the need to rationalise the departmental structure, placing emphasis on the need to achieve the corporate approach through more effective means of direction and co-ordination. To this end the following recommendations were made.

(*a*) A *chief executive officer* should be appointed to act as leader of the officer side of the authority and to act as principal adviser to the council on matters of general policy. The post would not be attached to any department.

(*b*) A *management team* should be established consisting of the principal chief officers of the authority, and should be formally recognised within the management structure. It would have responsibility under the chief executive officer for the preparation of plans and programmes in connection with the long-term objectives of the authority, and for the general co-ordination and implementation of these plans.

24. Response to the Bains Report. The response to the Bains Report has been as positive as that to the Maud Report was negative. The practical effect has been to apply the concept of corporate management through the great majority of local authorities. In particular there has been a move away from the traditional administration dichotomy of policy being reserved for the elected member and administration for the paid officer. The new organisation adopted recognises the role of officers in policy-making by institutionalising the management team and the chief executive officer as both co-ordinative and policy-making functionaries, whilst at the same time strengthening the member structure by rationalising the committee structure in order to avoid unnecessary conflict, and placing formal power in the hands of the policy and resources committee and its attendant resource committees, and retaining the council as the ultimate policy arbiter.

25. Conclusions. In general local government has now evolved a management structure which accepts the principles of the Bains Report as being basic to good management in local government. In particular the role of the chief executive officer is firmly established as is that of a central policy committee. It should be borne in mind however that local government is not amenable to a complete "management" approach for the following reasons.

(*a*) *Political reasons*. Theoretical management concepts which may be applicable to business organisations are subject to constraints in local government (*see* III). In particular British local government is as much a political as an administrative organisation, and any rationalisations implicit in management thinking must be applied against this background, e.g. the values of democratic control and administrative efficiency remain difficult to harmonise.

(*b*) *Participation*. Local government remains a field for participation by interested members of the community. Thus, increased efficiency is not accorded what theorists regard as its full due, as its implementation organisationally may reduce participation both by members and by outside organisations.

PROGRESS TEST 17

1. Outline the nature and problems of the traditional local government management structure. **(1–5)**

2. What are the basic requirements of management in local government? **(6)**

3. What comments did the Maud Committee on Management make on the existing local government management structure? **(7)**

4. What proposals did the Maud Committee make for reform? **(8, 9)**

5. What is meant by "city manager"? What are the advantages of the appointment? **(12, 13)**

6. What are the disadvantages of the use of the city manager system? Why is it considered inappropriate to English local government? **(14, 15)**

7. Outline other forms of North American management approach in local government. **(16)**

8. What problems face a chief executive officer? **(17)**

9. Examine the success of the application of the Maud recommendations. **(18)**

10. Explain the main provisions of the Bains Report, and comment why a "full management" approach is not appropriate to local administration. **(19–23)**

CHAPTER XVIII

Comparative Public Administration

FRANCE

1. Features. France has been referred to as a "civil service" or "administrative" state. Four dominant features may be identified in its system of public administration.

(*a*) The planning role of the government has been steadily increasing in regard to the national economy, and in this respect there is absence of clear demarcation between the public and private sectors.

(*b*) Freedom of executive action from the legislature's supervision and control was increased markedly under the Fifth Republic, and the executive is now firmly rooted in the Cabinet itself and in the President's staff.

(*c*) Policy is becoming increasingly the result of interaction between the administration and pressure groups, with a corresponding decline in the roles of the political parties and the legislature.

(*d*) Pressure-group activity is not filtered through the party machinery as in Britain, and consequently may work against the general public interest. In addition intra-administration groupings have developed, each seeking influence on administrative policy.

2. Organisation. The distinguishing features of French administrative organisation are as follows.

(*a*) The unity of the administrative machine.

(*b*) The dominance of the central machinery. This is not reduced by decentralisation of functions to local authorities and public corporations. These, though having a certain financial and administrative autonomy, do not have semi-independent status, as in the British system.

(*c*) The decentralisation of administrative functions. This results in the absence of a direct centre focus of administrative activity. French ministries operate through a complex system of regional and local branches, with many functional agencies concerned with keeping the minister in continuous contact with the localities.

(*d*) Co-ordination problems. These arise from this extensive decentralisation. Executive supervision is thus maintained through a network of personal secretariats, inspectorates, advisory committees, etc.

3. Central administration. This can be set out as follows.

(*a*) *The ministries*. Functional allocation tends to be much looser than that experienced in Britain. French ministries also vary from their British counterparts in the following ways.

(*i*) There is a greater emphasis on administrative deconcentration (only fifty-five per cent of ministry staffs are in Paris). They are thus more concerned with direct administration in the provinces, and do not rely on the British practice of semi-autonomous local agencies and officials.

(*ii*) Flexibility, manifested through reshuffling of functions and experimentation, is much greater than the comparatively rigid British practice.

(*iii*) There is greater use of technocracy (*see* VI). Specialist personnel are found to a much greater extent in advisory and policy-making roles. There is no general administrative class.

(*iv*) There is no figure comparable to a permanent secretary. The tendency to divisionalise departments (as in Britain) and to give each chief of "directions" direct responsibility to the minister is incompatible with the British practice of a co-ordinating head of department. This, however, gives rise to difficulties of co-ordination, and probably stems from the days of unstable parliamentary Cabinets.

(*b*) *Supervisory administration*. The French supervisory machinery has no comparison in Britain. It consists of the following bodies.

(*i*) A personal "Cabinet" (or secretariat) attached to each minister, inspectorate, and advisory council. These operate as the "eyes and ears" of the minister, as administrative co-ordinators and as ministerial supporters. They perform many of the functions of a permanent secretary, act as a form of "brains trust" and supervise the execution of ministerial policy.

(*ii*) Other supervisory and co-ordinating bodies include the inspectorate and advisory bodies. The inspectorate is composed entirely of civil servants and has wide investigatory powers in the field of the expenditure of public funds. In addition, it provides a pool of experience at the minister's disposal for special administrative or advisory functions.

The advisory bodies consist of two distinct groups i.e. those of a representative character and those entirely composed of civil servants. At the apex of the latter is the Economic and Social Council which operates to give interest and pressure groups a focal point and a formal access point to the French administrative system.

4. Council of State. This operates as a body giving technical advice to ministers on the drafting of legislation, and acts as an aid in planning and preparing the legislative programme. Its chief functions are thus planning, advising administration and resolving administrative difficulties. It must be consulted by the Prime Minister on all public administration matters and, though having no formal co-ordinating or control powers, is a body of considerable influence.

5. Nationalised industries and organisation for economic planning. French nationalised industries (*établissements publics*) have two distinctive features:

(*a*) they are treated as a part of the unitary state machinery;
(*b*) wide use is made of specialised representatives on boards.

NOTE: Because of (*a*) problems of control and responsibility associated with the British nationalised industries seldom arise.

The organisation for economic planning is formally headed by a planning commissioner with a planning commissariat. These have relatively little formal power but exercise wide influence through a network of agencies. Influence is exercised partly through the widespread operation of the National Plan and through membership of key agencies.

6. Local government. The integrated, unified nature of French central government results in a relatively weak local government organisation. Effectively it does not have the semi-independent status of the British and German systems (see **7**) but operates as part of the hierarchy of national planning, and thus tends to result in an intermixing of local and national responsibilities. Local services in fact are often administered through the field services of central ministries. Central power is highlighted by the weak financial circumstances of the French local government.

Local government is also denied independence by the role of the prefect who directs all state activities in his department and who exercises a powerful supervisory role (*tutelle administrative*) over local authorities.

NOTE: For a description of the French civil service *see* VI.

GERMANY

7. Introduction. Three major features of the German Federal Republic may be observed.

(*a*) Reliance is placed on executive leadership rather than on popular representation. This results in centralised and co-ordinated leadership, subject to the following two counterbalancing forces:

(*i*) the federal organisation of Germany;

(*ii*) the desire of social groups, etc., to have their interests represented in the executive.

(*b*) There is no genuine parliamentary system in the sense of enforceable executive responsibility to Parliament.

(*c*) The loose relationships between ministers and Parliament have strengthened the association of the political executive and the permanent bureaucracy. The absence of personal "Cabinets" or adequate parliamentary experience tends to place a minister greatly under the influence of the permanent bureaucracy, and gives the bureaucracy large measure of control of government and administration.

8. The ministries. These are generally functionally organised. However, the federal structure of the state has given rise to problems of division of functions between federal and *land* ministries. In many cases ministries have little administrative machinery or executive power, these being lodged with the different *länder* and their ministries.

The authority of the state is diffused down to its local agencies and, whilst obviating confusion of authorities and jurisdiction, means that society is permeated by the bureaucracy.

Little inter-departmental co-ordination machinery exists, and difficult problems of co-ordination thus arise which are accentuated by the practice of German executive branches forming separate parallel hierarchies, each with their own pattern of organisation.

9. Public enterprises. Most of such public activity is handled at local level and comparatively few public enterprises exist at federal level. A general *laissez-faire* approach exists with an accompanying absence of central planning.

10. The German civil service. The German civil service is noteworthy in that it provides a working example of the basic difficulty in public administration of reconciling democracy and efficiency. Civil servants have a high public status and the following characteristics.

(*a*) They are accorded "well-established rights".

(*b*) They are employed on a basis of technical merit. However, this does not imply completely open entry to the service and a form of cast system based on family, education, etc., exists under which only a comparative few have access to the service, particularly to the higher ranks.

(*c*) In return for long and expensive training, the German official is provided with security and status.

11. How satisfactory is the German system? The German civil servant is established for life, his agency is unchallenged, he is protected from publicity and investigation and he treats the post as an honour. This might be compared to the democratic position of the American civil service, where the civil servant is generally temporary, he needs to justify his work to the public and various committees, he functions under publicity and investigation and treats the post as "just another job".

The advantages of the system are that it contributes to the acquisition of a sense of duty, industriousness, to probity and to expert knowledge. On the other hand the German civil servant tends to be "authoritarian when left alone; resistant when under democratic direction; and conformist when under the direction of a forceful though untraditional ruling group such as the Nazis" (Fleidenheimer, *The Governments of Germany*, Methuen, 1961).

More objectively, the German civil service tradition is probably more appropriate to a static than to a dynamic state, and results in too compartmentalised attitudes.

12. Rejection of reform. Suggestions for open competition, restricted need for legal training, promotion from the ranks by specialist examination and the use of more persons with outside experience has been rejected. There is, however, a growth in the use of "functionary" officials, and the distinction of the English civil service between policy and administrative roles is not made.

13. Federal and land functions. The staff of most federal ministries is relatively small, and administration of federal programmes if often carried out by the *länder*, either as a matter of traditional prerogative or as a service rendered at the specific request of the federal government. There are thus four different ways in which administration is executed, namely:

(*a*) execution of federal laws by the federal administration, e.g. railways and the post office;

(*b*) execution of *land* laws by *land* administrations, e.g. police and education;

(*c*) execution of federal laws by *land* administration as a matter of right, e.g. labour and social welfare;

(*d*) execution of federal laws by the *land* administration at the request of the federal government, e.g. *autobahnen* and waterways.

14. Federal control. The federal government has extensive control over the *land* administration of federal laws. This is exercised through the giving of binding administrative regulations, demanding the rectification of inadequacies, and the use of investigatory agents. This tends to make the German federal system more unified than, say, the U.S.A. system, and this is reinforced by the general practice of *land* governments accepting federal administrative directions in order to further the general belief in the desirability of a relatively homogeneous system.

THE U.S.S.R.

15. The Soviet constitution. Superficially, the Soviet government resembles a typical Western European democracy in that the constitution provides for a national two-chamber legislature (i.e. the Supreme Soviet) with executive and administrative power vested in a council of ministers technically responsible to the

Supreme Soviet and the Presidium (i.e. the body representing the Supreme Soviet between its meetings). In practice, however, all these organs are controlled by the Communist party.

In addition, the federal system is designed to reflect the multi-racial character of the Soviet Union. In practice, however, it essentially represents a series of administrative units and not power divisions (compare the U.S.A.). This is the result of the existence of centrally-directed, all-embracing economic plans, and of the complete control of every area of the Union by the highly integrated and disciplined Communist party.

> NOTE: Concepts of freedom and democracy in the Soviet Union are basically different to western attitudes. Freedom is not conceived of in terms of representative and responsible government but in terms of economic welfare, breakdown of class divisions, etc.

16. The role and influence of the Communist party. The Communist party exists as a large pyramidal organisation, ranging from the base of over 300,000 primary party organisations to the apex of the Politburo, heading tightly integrated organs of power. The secretariat of the Central Committee is the supreme body for the preparation of plans and the making of policy. The central government is effectively an interlocking directorate, e.g. in 1978 Brezhnev was Premier of the Council of Ministers and Chairman of the Presidium as well as a member of the Politburo, as were the three first deputy Premiers.

The power of the political leaders is based on the following:

(a) control of party and administrative machines;
(b) the control of the propaganda machine;
(c) suppression of opposition.

17. Economic planning. Public administration is all-pervasive. The state, through its administrative agents, operates the whole economy. Economic planning has directed the growth of industry and now operates specific directions for the development of a state-owned and controlled economy. The status of economic planning was summed up by Stalin, who described economic plans as "instructions which are compulsory for all managements and which determine the future course of the economic development of the entire country" (G. M. Carter, *Government of the Soviet Union*, Harcourt, Brace & World Inc., 1965).

18. Structure of administration. Whilst not being subject to the constraints upon public administration found in Western democracies, the administrative structure in the Soviet Union gives rise to problems of co-ordination and direction wider in scope and different in character. It is based on the following.

(*a*) *Ministries, state committees and regional economic councils.* Ministries may take the form of "all Union" or "Union Republic", the latter directing the work of corresponding ministries at Union Republic level. All three organs carry out the basic work of direction and supervision and the heads of the ministries compose the Union Council of Ministers.

(*b*) *Administration of industry.* Features common to all organisation plans include the following:

(*i*) the breaking down of the industrial sector into segments with plans for each industry determined and co-ordinated at national level;

(*ii*) the use of "functional" bodies to deal with common needs;

(*iii*) territorial decentralisation of planning and operational powers.

NOTE: The administration of industry involves interaction of these three factors and considerable difficulty has been experienced in achieving machinery for smooth interaction.

19. The structure for planning. Planning in the Soviet Union involves three major tasks:

(*a*) the preparation of five-year plans;

(*b*) the preparation of the plans as detailed and unified entities for the economy and related fields, e.g. education;

(*c*) the determining of the supervisory structure which is able constantly to check the performance of all institutions involved in the plan.

There is, however, no clear pattern of planning agencies; e.g. the Gosplan's (state planning commission) functions have fluctuated in recent years. In 1955–6 it was responsible for long-range planning; from 1960–3 it was responsible for current policy. Long-term policy was returned to it in 1963 but at the same time a Supreme Council for the National Economy was established which is responsible for current policy.

20. Planning problems. The major planning difficulties have been as follows:

(*a*) preparing the plan and interrelating the different sector problems;

(*b*) putting the plan into operation and determining the authority which the relevant agencies need to execute the plan and take on-the-spot decisions.

In dealing with these tasks the planning machinery draws on the resources of a vast network of planning agencies.

(*a*) Territorially, each government area and sub-division has planning agencies.

(*b*) Functionally, there are planning agencies in every ministry and department, and also in every trust, factory and collective farm.

NOTE: The structure has an inbuilt inflexibility and change can only proceed slowly and within the framework of the overall plan.

21. Local level administration. The major local bodies are the local soviets. However, their position is more as agents of the central bureaucracy, owing to the pyramidal structure of the Soviet government. In addition, their functions may be usurped by large local industrial units. The purely local units of local government are administratively insignificant. The *oblasts* (regions) are no longer key economic units and *raions* (districts) are mainly used as organs for the retrieval of planning information.

Every administrative unit operates under a soviet and soviets are effectively controlled by the Communist party organisation.

22. Methods of administrative control. These are as follows.

(*a*) *Party controls.* The Communist party establishes a framework within which the administration must function. The party faction exists in each enterprise and branch of administration. The party thus provides the channels for securing detailed information on the workings of the economy, with counter-checking to ultimate levels.

(*b*) *The secret police.* This is a punitive as well as an investigatory body. It has been described as the ultimate symbol of "a system of power founded on the institutionalisation of mutual suspicion" (Merle Fainsod, quoted in G. M. Carter, *Government of the Soviet Union*, Harcourt, Brace & Wolff Inc., 1965).

(*c*) *Other controls.* Control is exercised also through the planning system, through centralised material supply and production and through agricultural procurement. This provides a centralised agency network, through which detailed administrative control on the working of the individual sectors of the economy is maintained.

23. The managers. No distinction is drawn between government officials and businessmen. The most important civil servants are the industrial managers who are chosen by the State Commission on the Civil Service. Training is technically and industrially orientated and no belief is placed in training in administrative techniques or cultural matters. Training, in practice, is effected through the training schools of the major administrative bodies.

THE U.S.A.

24. The central administration. The federal government consists of a multiplicity of agencies. This conglomerate can, however, be narrowed down to four principal types of institution.

(*a*) *Departments.* These were generally created out of bureaux or agencies operating in certain general areas. In general they will be of Cabinet rank and may often take the form of "holding companies" encompassing what in effect are several disparate functions. Examples of departments include State, Treasury and Defence.

(*b*) *Agencies.* These are effectively indistinguishable from departments and may attain Cabinet rank, e.g. National Aeronautical and Space Administration, National Labour Relations Board.

(*c*) *Independent commissions.* These developed with the growth of the regulatory function of government and, while originally being concerned with quasi-judicial functions, may now exercise important administrative tasks in their own right. They are usually constituted of three to eleven members appointed by the President subject to Senate approval. The principal administrative feature of the agencies is that they have created serious problems of co-ordination as their positive powers have developed. Examples of such commissions include the Civil Service Commission, the Commission on Civil Rights, etc.

(d) *Government corporations.* These are generally created in the U.S.A. to undertake specific functions, e.g. the Tennessee Valley Authority, the Export–Import Bank, etc.

25. Common features in the administration. The following factors often exist in common between the various departments, agencies, etc.

(a) *Political heads.* Each generally has a politically appointed head, usually on a partisan basis. Political appointments normally reach down to under and assistant secretary levels and to some of the subsidiary bureaux chiefs. In general, the head is responsible for policy and public relations and is supported by professional assistants men. Also grouped with him will be the various staff services, e.g. budget, planning. Below this level will be a series of bureaux executing the practical work of the department.

(b) *Field services.* These will generally be extensive and only a very small proportion of federal employees actually work in Washington. Such field services will be organised on a state basis or on regions of administrative convenience, though the state approach probably facilitates co-operation. Such deconcentration is not, however, unified and gives rise to problems of interdepartmental co-ordination and control problems, against which must be set the advantage of local differentiation and co-operation.

(c) *Consultation.* The departmental decision-making apparatus is supported by considerable consultation of interests. This machinery includes hearings, advisory committees and over four hundred inter-agency committees. The structure for consultation is both statutory-based and also results from spontaneous development.

(d) *Contracting.* All the agencies exercise the power to contract for the performance of their functions with other departments and extra-governmental agencies, e.g. in defence.

26. Nature of administration. Ernest S. Griffiths in *The American System of Government* (Methuen, 1976) has identified three features of bureaucratic development in the U.S.A., as follows.

(a) The acknowledgment of the vital role of research.

(b) The bureaucracy has to some extent achieved the status of the fourth branch of government and is as autonomous as Congress or the executive. It is thus a subject of checks and balances and fully shares a mutually interacting role with both the legislature and the executive (i.e. President and Cabinet).

(c) Bureaucracy has come to be characterised by the agency–clientele relationship. This results from the dispersive nature of the American society and the realisation of the importance of government intervention. This, in turn, has resulted in a tendency to express group objectives in legislation and for agencies to be set up to facilitate the achievement of such objectives, and thus brings about a close relationship between the government and the groups concerned. "The bureaucracy is not an unfaithful mirror of a dispersive society, but is considerably modified by the assumptions and symbols and rituals of the public interest under which it operates" (Ernest S. Griffith).

27. The civil service: background. The present federal civil service stems from the Civil Service Act 1883 (Pendleton Act), and the percentage of civil servants under the "classified-merit" rules has grown from 44.8 per cent in 1889 to 85.6 per cent by 1963.

There is an open competitive selection system of recruitment. However, the idea of a closed career service has been rejected and preference has been expressed for practical job-orientated selection and the availability of lateral entry to the service. This lateral entry approach (i.e. provision for recruitment from industry rather than promotion through the ranks) has had two side-effects, namely:

(a) it refreshes the bureaucracy with industrial and business intake;

(b) it may, however, frustrate the career developments of "career civil servants".

28. The civil service: use of specialists. There is a generally established pattern of use of specialist skills, and comparatively little opportunity for the "generalist" administrator (*see* VI). Specialist competence is in fact regarded as a prerequisite to administrative efficiency. Sixty-three bureau chiefs were studied by Michael E. Smith (Bureau Chiefs of the Federal Government, 1958, *Public Policy*, Vol. 10, 1960, Harvard University) in 1958; it appeared in general that they were appointed to jobs for which their education and previous experience were particularly relevant. Similarly, studies of the educational background of higher civil servants by W. Lloyd Warner (*The American Federal Executive*, Yale University Press, 1963) and David T. Stanley (*The Higher Civil Service*, Brookings Institution, 1964) have shown that emphasis was placed on physical science and engineering backgrounds rather than on a humanities-based education (compare British Administrative Class intake; *see* VI).

The role of the scientist in high positions was described by Don K. Price as follows: "if administration is to serve as a useful layer in the pyramid of policy between peak of political power and the base of science and technology", there is a need for high-ranking scientists, etc.

29. The civil service: a summing up. In conclusion, the following general elements of the federal civil service may be noted:

(*a*) the use of specialists in specified and administrative positions;

(*b*) the widespread practice of departments having to write detailed job specifications;

(*c*) the loss of image of a federal civil service and emphasis more on particular posts and activities;

(*d*) disregard of the utility of the career generalist administration;

(*e*) regular interchange with industry;

(*f*) regular inter-departmental movements.

30. Planning and co-ordination. The greatest problem of American government is the bringing together the disparate and comparatively independent agencies of government. It is beyond the scope of this book to deal fully with these, but the principal instruments of co-ordination may be summarised as follows.

(*a*) *The presidency.* This will include the use of such agencies as the Bureau of the Budget (*see* (*c*)), and the Council of Economic Advisers, as well as Cabinet members.

(*b*) *The bureaucracy.* Through the use of inter-departmental planning and co-ordinating committees.

(*c*) *Congress.* Appropriations, committees, control of the executive, etc.

NOTE: The Bureau of the Budget is the central control and co-ordinating agency. It is responsible for estimates, clearance of legislation, surveys of administrative efficiency and some central statistical control.

31. Conclusions. In drawing comparisons between various systems of public administration and relating them to the British system, thought must be used in extracting points which might be favourably employed. So many political, social, cultural and economic considerations underlie any national system of public administration that great care must be taken to avoid hasty cross-applications. However, the following points which could be utilised profitably in the British system, and certain points which should be avoided, can be listed:

(*a*) the value of professionalism, as typified by the American federal civil service;

(*b*) the nature and value of the training and education systems underlying the French national administration;

(*c*) the difficulties of co-ordination in totally planned economies, as shown by the experience of the U.S.S.R.;

(*d*) the dangers of inadequate political control, as expressed in the German system;

(*e*) the American use of consultation;

(*f*) the success of the French planning systems.

PROGRESS TEST 18

1. What are the principal features of French administration? **(1)**

2. Describe the major factors in the central administration of France. **(3)**

3. Consider the features of French administrative organisation for (*a*) the nationalised industries and (*b*) local government. **(5, 6)**

4. What are the principal administrative features of the German Federal Republic? **(7)**

5. Describe the general underlying features of the German civil service, and comment on its advantages. **(10–12)**

6. How are administrative functions divided up in Germany? How is federal control exercised over the *land* authorities? **(13, 14)**

7. How does the Communist party's role affect the working of the constitution of the U.S.S.R.? **(15, 16)**

8. Outline the structure of the administration in the U.S.S.R. **(18, 19)**

9. What are the principal methods of administrative control in the U.S.S.R.? **(22)**

10. Distinguish between the various agencies which form the central administration of the U.S.A. **(24)**

11. What common features in the central administration of the U.S.S.R. can be discerned? **(25)**

12. What basic features exist in the U.S.A. administration? **(26)**

13. Outline the main features of the civil service of the U.S.A. **(27–29)**

14. What conclusions may one draw from the study of foreign administrative systems? **(31)**.

Bibliography

Public administration theory
Brown, R. G. S., *The Administration Process in Britain*. University Press, 1971
Chapman, R. A. and Dunsire, A., *Style in Administration*. Allen and Unwin, 1971

Parliament
Stacey, Frank, *British Government, 1966–75*. Oxford University Press, 1975.

Government
Stankiewicz, W. J. (Ed.), *British Government in an Era of Reform*. Collier MacMillan, 1976
Wilson, Harold, *The Governance of Britain*. Sphere, 1977

Civil service
Chapman, R. A., *The Higher Civil Service in Britain*. Constable, 1970
Fry, C. K., *Statesmen in Disguise: the Changing Role of the Administrative Class of the Home Civil Service*. London, 1969

Examination Technique

Before the examination. It must be emphasised that the key to success in any examination lies in adequate preparation supplemented by constant revision. In particular, it is important to prepare for an examination from the outset of the course, and not to rely on last-minute cramming. In a subject such as public administration the importance of wide reading cannot be over-emphasised. This does not mean that a wide variety of books should be studied in detail but that the basic texts should be supplemented by a sound knowledge of the viewpoints put forward in specialist works.

At the examination. It may confidently be stated that a good student can undo months of careful preparation by ignoring certain simple basic rules of examination technique. In particular:

(*a*) Read with care the instructions on the examination paper.

(*b*) Write legibly and use good English.

(*c*) Read with utmost care the actual examination questions, remembering that marks will be lost for irrelevancy and that valuable time will be wasted.

(*d*) Allow spare time to plan in outline each answer and to divide all relevant points into clearly defined paragraphs.

(*e*) Do not panic if it is felt that excessive time is being spent on a particular question.

(*f*) Do not write for the sake of writing. Brevity with accuracy is absolutely preferable to a long and rambling discourse.

(*g*) In discussion questions be careful to give all points of view before settling on conclusions.

These notes are only intended as guidance, and it is appreciated that individuals may have developed their own personal examination techniques which suit them better.

Specimen Test Papers

Answer five questions. Time allowed: three hours.

PAPER 1

1. What, if anything, might be learnt from the selection and training of higher civil servants abroad which might improve the performance of the British civil service?

2. To what extent is it appropriate to be apply principles of management organisation derived from the private sector to public administrative organisation?

3. To what extent and in what ways does the House of Commons exercise control over government expenditure? Do you consider such control could be improved? If so, how?

4. What is meant by the sovereignty of Parliament? How far does such sovereignty apply at the present day?

5. "Any Minister must inevitably be under the control of the civil servants in his department." Discuss.

6. "In a democracy it would be disastrous if all citizens were politically active." Comment.

7. Although the concept of the specialist committee is an important part of the investigative process in most democratic legislatures, it has been accorded little significance in the British system.

8. Comment on this view and consider the desirability of extending the process. "Governments not parliaments make law." Discuss this assertion with respect to the British system of government.

PAPER 2

1. In what ways and with what possibilities of effectiveness does Parliament control the nationalised industries?

2. "There is no longer a valid case for civil service anonymity." Discuss.

3. Explain the theory and practice of the decision-making process in British public administration.

4. Although central departments and local authorities may be considered as administrative bodies, their powers and organisation are very different. Examine this statement.

5. What main defects in the civil service did the Fulton Committee attempt to rectify? What evidence is there of its success or otherwise?

6. On what basis are functions allocated between central departments. Explain why there has been a reaction against the concept of the "super department."

7. How are central departments co-ordinated both between themselves and at government level?

8. "The Prime Minister is an administrator who has little time, or excuse, to administer." Comment on the truth of this statement.

PAPER 3

1. To what extent is it possible in public administration to distinguish between policy-making and administration? Is any useful purpose served by attempting to differentiate the location of these functions?

2. Explain the meaning of "bureaucracy". To what extent may bureaucracy be said to be dysfunctional?

3. Do you consider there to be a case for the subordination of specialists to generalist administrators in public and local administration?

4. To what extent, if any, does the Central Policy Review Staff affect the relationship between ministers and civil servants? In what other ways might the position of the Minister be strengthened?

5. "The organisational structure of a body is less important than the interpersonal relationships within that body." "Without a scientifically derived structure discussion of human behaviour in organisations is irrelevant." Compare and discuss these comments.

6. "Enquiry into and the redress of citizens' grievances arising from maladministration is now so well developed that there need no longer be concern for the introduction of a new Bill of Rights." Discuss.

7. How may pressure groups in the U.K. be classified? Do you

consider the existence of such groups to be beneficial or detrimental in a democracy?

8. Comment on the structure and effectiveness of economic planning in the U.K.

Index

Details of some other Macdonald & Evans
HANDBOOKS on related subjects can be found on
the following pages.

For a full list of titles and prices write for the
FREE Macdonald & Evans Business Studies
catalogue, available from: Department BP1
Macdonald & Evans Ltd., Estover Road,
Plymouth PL6 7PZ

British Government and Politics
F. RANDALL

This HANDBOOK takes into account not only recent changes in the style and nature of government of Britain, but also the changes in the syllabuses of examining boards that set papers in British Constitution and Government, Government and Politics, Political Studies, and other related subjects. The text deals not only with the concepts of government and politics, and the institutions, but also political ideas and doctrines.

British Social Services
F. J. WRIGHT, *revised by* F. RANDALL

Since the first edition of this work appeared the pattern of social services in Britain has changed. Examinations and examining bodies have also changed, and the structure of this HANDBOOK has been adapted to meet the new situation and the altered needs of students in this wide and complex field.

Economics of Public Finance
EDMUND SEDDON

Written primarily for students taking the L.G.E.B. papers in Public Finance, this HANDBOOK deals with the theoretical and practical aspects of public finance and the general theory of price, and will be of great value to all students of economics. For this latest edition, in line with the shift in academic thinking, greater emphasis has been placed on the monetary implications of public finance.

Human Resources Management
H. T. GRAHAM

This HANDBOOK provides a framework for the study of human resources management, both for students of industrial psychology, personnel management and training and industrial relations, and for managers who wish to have a comprehensive reference book covering the human aspects of their work.

Local Government
MICHAEL P. BARBER

This HANDBOOK, designed for students preparing for examinations in local government administration, also provides the local government officer with an overall historical and structural picture to supplement his practical knowledge of his own work.

Meetings
L. HALL

This HANDBOOK will be invaluable to students seeking to master the details of meetings practice. For the latest edition the examination questions have been up dated.